500 Quotes From Heaven

*Life-Changing Quotes
That Reveal The Wisdom & Power
Of Near-Death Experiences*

David Sunfellow

Copyright © 2020 by David Sunfellow

All rights reserved.

David Sunfellow
P.O. Box 2242
Sedona, Arizona 86339 USA
quotesfromheaven.com

Cover design by David Sunfellow
Book layout © 2017 BookDesignTemplates.com

500 Quotes From Heaven
Life-Changing Quotes That Reveal
The Wisdom & Power Of Near-Death Experiences
David Sunfellow
ASIN: B08H5C9Z6Z
KDP ISBN: 9798673905678
Version 1.2

Dedicated to all the experiencers and researchers who gave us the life-changing words that fill these pages -- and to all the readers who will use these words to build new, more loving worlds.

"What we do now echoes in eternity."
Marcus Aurelius

And if we want our echo to be a joyous one:

"Love one another as I have loved you."
Jesus Christ

Contents

Introduction

1 – The History & Power Of Near-Death Experiences (1-16)
2 – Encounters With The Divine (17-73)
3 – Life Reviews: Loving, Learning, The Little Things (74-139)
4 – Lighten Up; Don't Take Life So Seriously (140-155)
5 – The Purpose Of Life (156-203)
6 – Everything Is Perfect (204-236)
7 – Delusions Of Grandeur (237-260)
8 – Paradise Lost (261-277)
9 – Suicide (278-293)
10 – Hell (294-335)
11 – Prayer (336-344)
12 – Angels (345-370)
13 – Nature (371-388)
14 – God, Jesus, Religion (389-421)
15 – Sex (422-429)
16 – Reincarnation (430-432)
17 – Drug-Induced Spiritual Experiences (433-441)
18 – The World Is A Dream (442-452)
19 – Apocalyptic Predictions (453-470)
20 – Creating Heaven On Earth (471-500)

Universal Truths
Experiencers & Researchers Featured In This Book
General NDE Resources
Topic-Specific NDE Resources
Notes

Introduction

By David Sunfellow

Reading this book cover to cover provides a comprehensive summary of the core truths championed by near-death experiences (NDEs) from around the world. It contains 500 of the most inspiring, instructive, and potent NDE quotes I have come across in over four and a half decades of research. Altogether, 129 near-death experiencers, 11 near-death-like experiencers, and 24 near-death experience researchers share their experiences, discoveries, and life-changing insights.

A list of the experiencers and researchers featured in this book, and the sections they are quoted in, can be found at the end of this book. The back of this book also includes links to source materials and important references, including a list of the world's foremost, most information packed NDE websites.

My previous book *The Purpose of Life as Revealed by Near-Death Experiences from Around the World* included some helpful advice I will repeat here:

Read this book slowly and carefully. There is so much power in these accounts that you might catch fire if you read them too fast.

Or you might miss out.

Whether you are new to the subject of near-death experiences, or have studied them for decades, reading these accounts is akin to being struck by lightning. Repeatedly. Not only do they communicate universal truths with unparalleled clarity and power, but they also make it crystal clear how to apply these truths to our daily lives, which is what I care most about.

NDE Researcher Kenneth Ring said it best:

"The true promise of the NDE is not so much what it suggests about an afterlife -- as inspiring and comforting as those glimpses are -- but what it says about how to live NOW... to learn from NDErs about how to live, or how to live better, with greater self-awareness, self-compassion, and concern for others."

-One-
The History & Power Of Near-Death Experiences

Near-death experiences have shaped human history from the beginning of time. It is only now, after acquiring the ability to collect and analyze NDEs from around the world, that we are realizing just how deeply these experiences have influenced humankind, past and present...

1

Our situation regarding near-death experiences is similar to the way humanity learned of exotic lands during the ancient era of exploration. After sailors returned from long voyages and wrote their accounts, scholars would survey multiple accounts from different voyagers, discern where they agreed or disagreed, and come up with the most likely descriptions of the geography, culture, rituals, and traditions of a particular exotic land. We are in a similar position today when it comes to the world of the afterlife.

-- Near-Death Experience Researcher Jeffrey Long, MD

2

Near-death experiences are surprisingly common. A Gallup poll found that about five percent of those surveyed had an NDE at some time during their lives. From this and other surveys, we believe that millions of people around the world have had near-death experiences.

-- Near-Death Experience Researcher Jeffrey Long, MD

3

NDEs and similar altered states of consciousness occur in all cultures. A survey by George Gallup and William Proctor undertaken in 1980-81 estimated that eight million Americans had experienced an NDE. Since then, with advances in medical technology, that figure has probably markedly increased as more people are surviving critical illness. A survey published in 2005 estimated that eight percent of the Australian population has experienced an NDE. Australian NDEs are consistent with other Western NDEs. A study conducted in 2001 showed that four percent of a sample of German people reported an NDE, which gives an estimate of three million Germans who have experienced an NDE.

-- Near-Death Experience Researcher Penny Sartori, PhD

4

The results of the Near-Death Experience Research Foundation (NDERF) study finds that what people discovered during their near-death experience about God, love, afterlife, reason for our earthly existence, earthly hardships, forgiveness, and many other concepts is strikingly consistent across cultures, races, and creeds. Also, these discoveries are generally not what would have been expected from preexisting societal beliefs, religious teachings, or any other source of earthly knowledge.

-- Near-Death Experience Researcher Jeffrey Long, MD

5

Even after rigorously studying NDEs for over fifteen years, I still marvel at how amazingly similar these experiences are regardless of the experiencers' age, cultural beliefs, education, or geographical location. By comparing these accounts, we begin to see a coherent picture of this other world.

-- Near-Death Experience Researcher Jeffrey Long, MD

6

It is now clear that [near-death experience] accounts can be found in humankind's earliest writings, including the Bible, Plato's Dialogues, the Egyptian Book of the Dead, and the

Tibetan Book of the Dead. As that list of texts suggests, it is also now known that NDEs have been described across cultures, not only in the literature of Western culture but also in the folklore of Native American, South Pacific Islander, and East and Central Asian cultures and in the literature of non-Western cultures. Indeed, accounts of near-death and out-of-body experiences can be found in the oral traditions and written literature of about 95 percent of the world's cultures.

-- Near-Death Experience Researchers Janice Miner Holden, EdD, Bruce Greyson, MD, Debbie James, MSN

7

Until the late twentieth century, historically and historiographically, near-death experiences were neglected experiences. Considering the sheer volume of documentary narratives alongside related myths, practices, and beliefs as found in the anthropological record, this is surprising ... What has prevented them from being identified as a discreet and important class of phenomenon by the vast majority of anthropologists and other interpreters of religions? Indeed, what has prevented such a relevant experience type from being seen as a factor contributing to religious beliefs, to the extent that serious arguments to this effect have been isolated, rare, or effectively marginalized?

The answer would seem to lie in a refusal to take indigenous testimony seriously, from early missionary astonishment that afterlife beliefs could derive from NDEs, to philosophical and religious denigrations of the authority of experience, to Mircea Eliade's determined obsession with universalizing shamanism, to medical and psychological pathologization, to postmodernist fixations on the particularities of culture and language to the exclusion of all else. All these perspectives deny a voice to the very people whose religions and experiences are being "explained" (or, rather, **explained away**).

-- Scholar and Near-Death Experience Researcher Gregory Shushan

8

[The spiritual traditions and practices of Native Americans provide] a virtual model of the experiential source hypothesis: that NDEs as filtered through cultural/individual layers are commonly the basis of afterlife beliefs. There are nearly seventy narratives describing . . . Native American NDEs across the continent, dating from the late sixteenth to early twentieth centuries. More than twenty overt indigenous statements testify that local Native American afterlife beliefs, and even whole religious movements, commonly originated in NDEs.

-- Scholar and Near-Death Experience Researcher Gregory Shushan

9

Based on the groundbreaking work of scholars like Gregory Shushan, it is now clear that near-death experiences provided the source material that both civilized and indigenous cultures built their spiritual traditions on. What's more, an evolutionary impulse has provided a constant stream of new NDEs, with increasingly refined information, that has caused cultures around the world to modify old beliefs and practices and adopt new ones. In other words, near-death experiences have been teaching, healing, guiding, and evolving humankind from the earliest days. What's different today, is that we finally have the tools -- and awareness -- to recognize this remarkable fact.

-- Near-Death Experience Researcher David Sunfellow

10

While near-death experiences have profoundly influenced human beings and human history since the beginning, in recent decades they have turned into a global phenomenon. Whereas most spiritual paths, religions, and philosophical movements trace back to one visionary, modern near-death experiences are now being reported by millions of people all over the world -- children and old people, rich and poor, educated and illiterate, believers and non-believers, atheists and materialists. The heavens are literally pouring down on us, providing us with so much data that we now have the ability to not only collect this information, but actually separate, to a large degree, the universal themes of these experiences from the personal and cultural conditioning they come wrapped in. The only other universal experience I am aware of that comes close to matching the consistent universality of NDEs are non-dual states of consciousness. Dreams, visions, out-of-body experiences, kundalini awakenings, shamanic experiences, channelings, UFO encounters, hypnotic regressions, and other spiritually transformative experiences are also universal experiences, but they tend to contain less voltage, consistency, and clarity than NDEs.

-- Near-Death Experience Researcher David Sunfellow

11

Near-death experiences are not only coming to us as a universal revelation, but they also contain serious firepower. Whereas other religious, spiritual, and philosophical systems (and other kinds of paranormal experiences) may (or may not) have the power to change lives for the better, NDEs are consistently packed with reality-defying miracles of all kinds. There is no other human experience that delivers profoundly changed lives so consistently. I think that's why NDEs have generated so much interest. We intuit that there is something about NDEs that is akin to angels knocking on our personal and collective doors. While people are still trying to deny the evidence of their presence, the NDE angels are becoming increasingly difficult to ignore, shoo away, or dismiss as the product of malfunctioning brains. Something new and important is happening here.

-- Near-Death Experience Researcher David Sunfellow

12

We live in a community in which many people have different political opinions, values, religious beliefs, and lifestyles than ourselves . . . In our experience, near-death experiences have the power to unite us as no other topic can, and to help us form immediate heart and soul connections with people to whom we might otherwise struggle to relate.

-- Near-Death Experience Researchers Sheila, Dennis, and Matthew Linn

13

In one of my visits with The Light I was told that the near-death experience would become more and more popular and it would have an effect on the entire world when a critical mass was hit and all these people have died and come back and are telling you that there is a lot more going on than we think.

-- Near-Death Experiencer Mellen-Thomas Benedict

14

One of my guides said, "We have placed people like you (near-death experiencers) in specific locations to be funnels for that connection to heavenly love; to be that Source of Divine Love on this planet." I felt like that was a big job and that's a big reason I came back.

-- Near-Death Experiencer Nancy Rynes

15

The larger meanings of NDEs: May it be that NDErs -- and others who have had similar awakenings -- collectively represent an evolutionary thrust toward higher consciousness for humanity at large? Could it be that the NDE itself is an evolutionary mechanism that has the effect of jump-stepping individuals into the next stage of human development by unlocking spiritual potentials previously dormant? Indeed, are we seeing in such people -- as they mutate from their pre-NDE personalities into more loving and compassionate individuals -- the prototype of a new, more advanced strain of the human species striving to come into manifestation? No longer Homo sapiens perhaps, but tending toward what John White has called Homo noeticus? Could NDErs be, then, an evolutionary bridge to the next step in our destiny as a species?

-- Near-Death Experience Researcher Kenneth Ring, PhD

16

It is high time we stop being merely mesmerized and intrigued by NDE stories and start putting their profound, powerful, and practical lessons into practice.

-- Near-Death Experience Researcher Jeff Janssen

- Two -
Encounters With The Divine

Direct encounters with The Divine change people in dramatic and unexpected ways. After discovering how intensely they are loved by The Divine, many experiencers become one with God and see, feel, and know everything God does. When they return to this world, many report miraculous healings. Most experiencers also discover that they have been transformed into new people with enhanced abilities, including psychic and paranormal powers...

17

The Light welcomed me; The Light absorbed me into The Light. So I was part of The Light. Once I was in The Light, I knew everything The Light knew. I knew all about the universe. I knew everything about flowers, plants, asteroids, suns, novas -- everything. I didn't have a question for The Light. Why? Because I knew all the answers. I had nothing to ask.

-- Near-Death Experiencer Andy Petro

18

I was given total and absolute knowledge about ALL things instantaneously! I marveled in ecstasy that I knew everything about everything there was to know in the universe right then and there. It was incredibly energizing to comprehend all that power, from knowledge about physics, astronomy, psychology, medicine, agriculture, meteorology, chemistry -- EVERYTHING about how the physical and spiritual worlds operate. I felt electrifying elation, being "on top of the world", and so joyful to possess ultimate Truth.

-- IANDS Near-Death Experiencer #1

19

In time, the questions ceased, because I suddenly was filled with all the Being's wisdom. I was given more than just the answers to my questions; all knowledge unfolded to me, like the instant blossoming of an infinite number of flowers all at once. I was filled with God's knowledge, and in that precious aspect of His Beingness, I was one with Him.

-- Near-Death Experiencer Beverly Brodsky

20

I was aware of everything that had ever been created. It was like I was looking out of God's eyes. I had become God. Suddenly I wasn't me anymore. The only thing I can say, I was looking out of God's eyes. And suddenly I knew why every atom was, and I could see everything.

-- Near-Death Experiencer Mellen-Thomas Benedict

21

In that other "dimension" I was suddenly aware of EVERYTHING -- all the connections, all the "whys" and the answers to the whys of my former life. It's as if all this life I had been in a state of half awareness, or amnesia, wandering around asking "Who I am? Why am I? Why is this so hard? Why? Why? Why?" and in that other realm the picture was finally complete. I got all the answers, or I remembered all the answers.

-- Near-Death Experiencer Amphianda Baskett

22

I felt as if I were at the center of the Universe with a complete panoramic view in all directions. The next instant I began to feel a forward surge of movement. The stars seemed to fly past me so rapidly that they formed a tunnel around me. I began to sense awareness, knowledge. The farther forward I was propelled the more knowledge I received. My mind felt like a sponge, growing and expanding in size with each addition. The knowledge came in single words and in whole idea blocks. I just seemed to be able to understand everything as it was being soaked up or absorbed. I could feel my mind expanding and absorbing and each new piece of information somehow seemed to belong. It was as if I had known already but forgotten or mislaid it, as if it were waiting here for me to pick it up on my way by. I kept growing with knowledge, evolving, expanding and thirsting for more . . . As each second passed, there was more to learn, answers to questions, meanings and definitions, philosophies and reasons, histories, mysteries, and so much more, all pouring into my mind. I remember thinking, "I knew that, I know I did. Where has it all been?"

-- Near-Death Experiencer Virginia Rivers

23

I could think on several levels at once and communicate them all simultaneously. You can't know something without knowing everything around it, what causes it, what sustains it. Knowledge dovetails in the spirit world, each piece fitting with other pieces. Every fact connected to it is seen instantly, in totality. We have nothing like it on Earth.

-- Near-Death Experiencer RaNelle Wallace

24

In this place, whatever it is, I did not have the limited consciousness I have on Earth. It felt like I had 125 senses to our normal five. You could do, think, comprehend, and so on, you name it, with no effort at all. It's as if the facts are right before you in plain sight with no risk of misinterpretation because the truth just is! Nothing is hidden. Communication is done by your thinking, your question and answer. Well-formed thoughts would just pop into your mind and you would know it came from another source. You would project your own thoughts that way, too. In this other realm, things like truths were just there before you, and all you had to do was just think of what you wanted to know and there it was. The mind was paramount, and one thing that astonished me was my ability to think as many things as I liked all at the same time. I can remember how stunned I was when I realized I was thinking many, many thoughts at the same time with complete comprehension and ease.

-- Near-Death Experiencer Peggy

25

I saw and knew that the Cosmos is not dead matter but a living Presence, that the soul of man is immortal, that the universe is so built and ordered that without any peradventure all things work together for the good of each and all, that the foundation principle of the world is what we call love, and that the happiness of everyone in the long run is absolutely certain. I learned more within the few seconds that illumination lasted than in all my previous years of study and I learned much that no study could ever have taught.

-- Near-Death-Like Experiencer Richard Maurice Bucke

26

I remember thinking, "Wow, now I get it! Everything about our existence finally makes sense!" The transference of information was immense and reassuring. [My guide] kept saying, "All is known. You have simply forgotten."

-- Near-Death Experiencer Laurelynn Martin

27

He said to me that I was in a different "place", one in which communication was purely exchanged through the language of love. Here everyone spoke heart to heart and soul to soul so that there could never be a misunderstanding. When I had been on Earth and used the spoken word, there had often been great confusion as to what I thought I had said and what had been heard by my listener, they were often very different.

-- Near-Death Experiencer Laura M

28

The quality of His word, His thought, His voice in my head, was magnificent, enchanting, compelling without demand, gentle and kind and filled with more love than is possible to describe. To be in His presence was more inspiring, more inviting, than any kind of love or harmony ever discovered in this reality. No experience, no closeness has ever been so complete.

-- Near-Death Experiencer Virginia Rivers

29

A voice boomed so loudly that it could make the universe explode. It said: "Everything is one. There is no past. There is no future. There is only now. And not only that, but every possible outcome, for every possible situation, is occurring at the same time."

The last statement I couldn't quite understand. I was shown an example of being at an intersection behind the wheel of a car and going straight, turning right, turning left, hitting the building on the corner, hitting a light post, going straight up into the air, burrowing into the asphalt -- all at the same time. Every possibility was occurring at the same instant whether I did it or not.

Then I heard, "The largest of the large and the smallest of the small are the same." I became a wave, a spiral, or a tube of sorts that contracted and expanded in and out with the "in" being microscopic and the "out" being infinitely large. I understood to the depths of my being that everything was one and that the smallest atom is the same as the universe. I was turned inside out and became everything, and everything was as tiny as the smallest particle and as huge as the universe. It was all the same, and I was it, and it was me.

I was just there, floating in this pure ecstasy, knowing to the depths of my being everything I had just heard and witnessed. Suddenly, I was being downloaded with information about every question I had ever had. I have always been interested in science, physics, biology, human relations, spirituality, religion, etc. In one instant, I understood all there was to know. I particularly remember understanding all about how electricity works, then physics, then human relationships.

[I felt] pure joy, and a feeling of simplicity. Then an understanding that it's all love. Everything is love. Everything is one. Everything is now.

-- IANDS Near-Death Experiencer #2

30

The Light flooded my consciousness with ultimate knowledge. I knew everything there was to know -- past, present, and future. Every word and thought that was or ever will be spoken or written was made known to me. I was not permitted to remember all that knowledge upon my return to the physical dimension, however, only parts of it.

-- Near-Death Experiencer Nancy Clark

31

I knew everything about the universe: why, how, what's the point of it all? I was there for so long, it was hard not to know everything! When I returned, I couldn't remember a lot of information that I had received. I assumed it was intentional.

-- IANDS Near-Death Experiencer #3

32

People who have had near-death experiences, I have since learned, have described encounters with The Light as being exposed to complete knowledge. Yet when they are asked what they remember, they recall few if any specifics. That's the way it was for me. At the time, I felt I was in touch with everything, but subsequently, I couldn't recall the knowledge.

-- Near-Death Experiencer Howard Storm

33

I have interviewed many near-death experiencers who reentered this lifetime cured of the physical illnesses that caused their deaths. I have painstakingly reviewed their complete hospital medical records. My cases include people who have come back totally healed of kidney failure, end-stage liver failure, aplastic anemia (bone marrow shutdown), legal blindness, pneumonia, and cancer. I have also interviewed several people who, after being pronounced dead by trained medical personnel, were in that state for a very long time. Three people awoke in the hospital morgue. Another person reentered his life in a funeral parlor.

-- Near-Death Experience Researcher Barbara Rommer, MD

34

I have had doctors telling me, over and over, that what happened to me is completely unexplainable. Medically, it should not be possible. They can't figure out where the billions of cancer cells went in just a matter of days. Medically, every way they look at it, I should have died. My organs were shut down. Either the cancer should have killed me, the drugs should have killed me, or the billions of cancer cells trying to leave, flooding my shut down system, should have killed me... The word "impossible" has no meaning to me anymore.

-- Near-Death Experiencer Anita Moorjani

35

Because of my experience, I am now sharing with everyone I know that miracles are possible.

-- Near-Death Experiencer Anita Moorjani

36

I was in a drug-induced coma; on a respirator and life support, after a pulmonary hemorrhage caused by severe lupus. I also had organ (kidney) failure and traumatic brain injury due to oxygen deprivation. I was not expected to live, but I came back completely healed from my lupus after my NDE. I have been totally well since, with no trace of Lupus since 2005. I was sent back well!

-- Near-Death Experiencer Anne N

37

Mellen-Thomas Benedict was part of my original research base. My husband and I personally journeyed to his home, and spent a great deal of time with him, some with his mother and then girlfriend. I've followed his work ever since . . . I can say point-blank that his near-death episode is genuine. I have viewed the before and after X-rays of his brain. The tumor was clearly there before he died; it disappeared after he revived. His is certainly not the only such case of instantaneous healing after a near-death experience. There have been many. Some far more dramatic than his.

-- Near-Death Experiencer and Researcher P.M.H. Atwater

38

Rosemary Ringer had been diagnosed with stage 2 cervical cancer when, after a routine medical procedure, she ended up bleeding to death, during which she had an intense near-death experience. Assured by angels during her sojourn in the afterlife, Rosemary had a complete remission of cancer and rapidly healed from her medical trauma. She also had a healing from the grief of her husband's earlier suicide. This profound NDE led her to completely transform her life. Rosemary adds: "After I was out of the hospital, I realized that the arthritis that had plagued me in my wrist, disappeared. I had a busted knee from an old injury that healed up. I had a busted shoulder from an old injury . . . My friend in IT said, 'You got rebooted by The Creator!' "

-- Near-Death Experiencer Rosemary Ringer

39

Annabel Beam was five years old when she was diagnosed with two rare life-threatening digestive disorders, pseudo-obstruction motility disorder and antral hypomotility disorder, which resulted in frequent hospital stays. When she was 10 years old, Annabel fell headfirst inside an old, hollowed-out tree. While unconscious inside the tree, with rescue workers struggling to get to her, she visited heaven and met Jesus. Jesus told her: "I have plans for you to complete on Earth that you cannot complete in Heaven. It's time for you to go back, and the firemen are going to get you out of the tree and when they do, you will be totally fine. There will be nothing wrong with you." After surviving the fall and rescue without a scratch, Annabel was inexplicably cured of her chronic ailments.

-- Near-Death Experiencer Annabel Beam

40

The NDE had a sort of physical healing with me. Physical problems that haunted me all my life disappeared afterward. These problems were chronic migraine headaches, for which I had to take pills for years, cramps, and a terribly anxious stomach, which would act up before school every day, soccer games, tests, and in just about all social situations. Before my experience I was the most klutzy, accident-prone fool you could have ever met. All these problems were solved through my NDE.

-- Near-Death Experiencer Neev

41

Suddenly, not knowing how or why, I returned to my broken body. But miraculously, I brought back the love and the joy. I was filled with an ecstasy beyond my wildest dreams. Here, in my body, the pain had all been removed. I was still enthralled by a boundless delight. For the next two months, I remained in this state, oblivious to any pain. I felt now as if I had been made anew. I saw wondrous meanings everywhere; everything was alive and full of energy and intelligence.

-- Near-Death Experiencer Beverly Brodsky

42

People who have had NDEs tend to be especially sensitive to their physical environment after they return. They are less able to tolerate anything that is inconsistent with the intensely vital, life-giving energy of the other realm. Thus, they have more adverse reactions to pharmaceuticals, other drugs, and alcohol than previously. Many avoid foods that contain chemicals or artificial sweeteners and prefer organic foods instead. Some become vegetarians. They seek out nature and fresh air. This sensitivity extends to sounds. Many NDEs include music, and NDErs typically feel drawn to music that resonates with their experience. They prefer natural, gentle, melodious sounds and take more pleasure than before in classical or soothing music. They dislike loud, jarring noise.

-- Near-Death Experiencer Researchers Sheila, Dennis, and Matthew Linn

43

After eight years, people with an NDE scored significantly higher in the following areas: showing emotions; less interest in the opinion of others; accepting others; compassion for others; involvement in family; less appreciation of money and possessions; increase in the importance of nature and environment; less interest in a higher standard of living; appreciation of ordinary things; sense of social justice; inner meaning of life; decline in church attendance; increased interest in spirituality; less fear of death; less fear of dying; and increase in belief in life after death. These different levels of change are a consequence of the NDE and not of surviving a cardiac arrest.

-- Near-Death Experience Researcher Pim van Lommel, MD

44

There is a deeper love and unity with everyone and everything that I come in contact with. I seem to have a greater awareness of all living things and that we are ALL a part of one another and ultimately a part of a greater consciousness, God. For the first time in my life, my earthly eyes have opened to see -- really see -- life around me. The simplest sights, a leaf, a tree, a blade of grass, a frog -- EVERYTHING is a marvel of creation to me and I take the time to appreciate it because I feel the bond of life between us.

-- Near-Death Experiencer Nancy Clark

45

Many people ask how my life is different after my NDE. I am happier and more at peace. Many things that bothered me before don't bother me now. In situations where I might get mad at someone in the past, I now see their reason for doing what they did. I am not afraid of dying or of hell anymore. I enjoy life, instead of worrying about what others think of me. My experience taught me how to treat people, not through rules or guidelines, but simply based on the love I feel within. I feel more compassion for other people and so much more empathy. Although I never liked hurting anyone's feelings before, that feeling is now much stronger. I don't like telling a lie and can't tell one without feeling like a piece of shit afterwards.

-- Near-Death Experiencer Chris Batts

46

I instantly changed from a pessimist to an optimist. There always seemed to be a brighter side to everything. I knew that everything happened for a reason. Sometimes, that reason may not have been clear at first, but in the end, it would all make sense.

-- Near-Death Experiencer Neev

47

[After my NDE], my dependence on time seemed to stop. I no longer felt pressured by the clock -- there was always time to do something else or more. I tried to fit in as much as possible into every day.

-- Near-Death Experiencer Neev

48

I was no longer interested in what "society" had to say about how I lived my life. I was no longer interested in what people thought or how they felt about me, or if I looked good or not. I learned that I am much more than my body.

-- Near-Death Experiencer Neev

49

My feeling of warmth and love flew through from my body and brought me many new friends. I felt comfortable in groups of people to the point that I needed to be surrounded by them. I had no fears of rejection or embarrassment. These were trivial things that had no consequence in the larger scheme of things.

-- Near-Death Experiencer Neev

50

I realized my mortality, unlike most of my friends. The closeness I had with death kept me from foolishly toying with life, mine and others, like I had before. In learning of my mortality, I also learned to accept death, and in a weird way, I look forward to it.

-- Near-Death Experiencer Neev

51

I do not fear many things anymore. Instead, I accept them for what they are and apply them to my life. I tend to try new things more readily, since I want to make the most of my new life without missing a thing.

-- Near-Death Experiencer Neev

52

Many of the things I valued previously seemed virtually unimportant to me. Money and material objects were not even a secondary thought to me. I became very generous with all of my time and material things. I joined several school philanthropy groups and spent time working in several soup kitchens. The most major change I noticed in myself was the loss of the desire to compete. Competition was the major driving force in my life before my NDE, but afterward, it seemed foolish and unimportant. Sports were still fun, but I lost that killer instinct that helped me get recruited by several universities.

-- Near-Death Experiencer Neev

53

Neev found that he had acquired the ability to reenter that otherworldly state during sleep, where he could, in effect, rehearse actions and test their effects before actually performing them in the physical world.

-- Near-Death Experience Researcher Kenneth Ring, PhD, commenting on the aftereffects reported by Neev

54

Neev also seemed to develop an extended range of intuitive and psychic perception that sometimes permitted him to know or sense the outcome of events before they took place.

-- Near-Death Experience Researcher Kenneth Ring, PhD, commenting on the aftereffects reported by Neev

55

[The enhanced empathic ability I acquired after my NDE] allows me to empathize with almost anyone. I feel that when I talk to people, I can physically and emotionally feel what they are going through at that time. It is as if I become them for an instant . . . The gift of insight allows me to help many people with their problems, but sometimes [it] gets to the point where there are so many that I lose myself in other people.

-- Near-Death Experiencer Neev

56

My ability to see the future, and my tendency to react and answer the private thoughts and intentions of my father's business associates, rather than their outward, polished manners, was very disturbing to everyone. I had to retrain myself to listen and think on two levels -- face value and true feelings. Unless I was on guard, I would respond to questions by answering what was in the person's inner thoughts and motives, rather than to the face value of their words.

-- Near-Death Experiencer Steve

57

I found I could memorize and play a Bach prelude and fugue with only a few hours of preparation, whereas before I had to struggle for weeks to learn a piece of music.

-- Near-Death Experiencer Steve

58

At twenty-six, I started buying books and learning languages. First French, then Spanish. After two semesters, I started on Don Quixote and read Voltaire's Philosophical Letters. Then, I returned to Portuguese [he had previously lived in Brazil]. At twenty-eight, I studied history and philosophy. At twenty-nine, I began excursions into particle physics and electronics. At thirty-two, I started designing oscillators and low-noise amplifiers. One of them is in an orbiting satellite. At thirty-six, I started designing microprocessors. I'm forty-two now. As a professional programmer, I write about 40,000 lines of C-language a year... I went through most of them. They were on history, philosophy, other religions, astronomy, physics, and archeology. Excepting masterworks and classics, I don't read fiction anymore.

-- Near-Death Experiencer Steve

59

I left my marriage as soon as I could walk again. I experienced ongoing mystical states of consciousness to the point of greatly disrupting my life. I began sensing other people's emotions and physical states. I dropped birth control and influenced my fertility instead through communicating with my unborn children. I experienced major, major neuroendocrine changes, major electrical disruption to the point I had to stop wearing a watch and many holistic medical tests that rely on the electricity of the body do not work on me. Healer after healer in various modalities said they had never seen what they saw was happening in my body. I got stopped on the street more than once to be asked what the light was around my head, or from light healers who just wanted to make contact. I dropped western medicine -- despite a shattered pelvis, my children were born at home because they made it clear to me ahead of time that's how it would be safest and healthiest for all of us. My sexuality/libido radically shifted and orgasms began to fill the room around me rather than my body. My family shifted from a middleclass normal house to giving our belongings away and living on the road, following intuition rather than society's shoulds.

-- Near-Death Experiencer Cami Renfrow

60

I was an atheist before I had my near-death experience. I still don't follow any religion, but my intuitive skills, my clairvoyance, my ability to see through the bullshit and the lies and the illusion is unbelievable. It has been like this since I came back.

-- Near-Death Experiencer Julie Aubier

61

I have very unique and close relationships with animals. I have actually been asked to leave the Toronto Zoo because all of the animals I passed came over to stand in front of me in their enclosures. Many pressed themselves right up against the bars or glass and tried to touch me . . . People and animals have even followed me home for no discernible reason other than to be with me. I have grown used to this behavior, and I no longer question it. I also appear to have a VERY green thumb, and plants that florists have declared as dead come to life for me. I just seem to know intuitively what to do.

-- IANDS Near-Death Experiencer #4

62

I felt pleasure, immense peace, a love that I have never felt. I felt complete in myself, fulfilled. Everything made sense. I was finally able to unite all the threads of my existence and understand that for which I had been created and why I was here. I felt an immense love for everyone that was here. I adored the animals, and all creation. From that moment on I could never see suffering of an animal or think that the trees and plants didn't have feelings. I felt that everything had a harmonious feeling.

-- Near-Death Experiencer Ana Cecilia G

63

I would come to myself and lie awake for about an hour, but in an utterly transformed state. It was as if I were in an ecstasy. I felt as though I were floating in space, as though I were safe in the womb of the universe in a tremendous void but filled with the highest possible feeling of happiness. "This is eternal bliss," I thought. "This cannot be described; it is far too wonderful!" Everything around me seemed enchanted . . . Night after night I floated in a state of purest bliss.

-- Near-Death Experiencer Carl Jung

64

I would never have imagined that any such experience was possible. It was not a product of imagination. The visions and experiences were utterly real; there was nothing subjective about them; they all had a quality of absolute objectivity.

-- Near-Death Experiencer Carl Jung

65

After the illness [that included Jung's near-death experience] a fruitful period of work began for me. A good many of my principal works were written only then. The insight I had had, or the vision of the end of all things, gave me the courage to undertake new formulations. I no longer attempted to put across my own opinion but surrendered myself to the current of my thoughts. Thus, one problem after the other revealed itself to me and took shape.

-- Near-Death Experiencer Carl Jung

66

After my near-death experience, I stood at a crossroads. Either A) everything I had ever believed about a godless universe was wrong or B) I'd had a drug trip. I chose B. That way, I could continue the life I knew of drinking and chasing popularity. So I locked my NDE away in a vault . . . After a series of paranormal events . . . the last pillar of my atheism toppled. It took 21 years for me to fully align with what I experienced during my near-death experience.

-- Near-Death Experiencer Louisa Peck

67

The Light told me everything was Love, and I mean everything! I had always felt love was just a human emotion people felt from time to time, never in my wildest dreams thinking it was literally EVERYTHING!

-- Near-Death Experiencer Peggy

68

One day when I was in Manhattan for a few days of work, I went out for a long walk and I prayed. I began to feel the spirit of peace, of contentment and presence that I feel when I walk in the woods and I realized that it was coming from the people around me on the sidewalks. They were nature and radiating the presence of [God] as a tree would, as stone might, as a songbird's song does. I walked for hours through the mass of humanity as if immersed in the wilderness where the spirit of God is strongest.

-- Near-Death Experiencer Peter Panagore

69

I don't know how, but I could see the smallest, tiniest particle. What the universe is made out of. It was this massive, uniform field of particles. At the tiniest level, the tiniest particle, smaller than anything we can record, it was pure white, sort of a radiant light. This particle was pure energy. But more than that, this particle that everything in the entire universe is made out of, is LOVE! A tangible love that is the stuff of God. It just blew me away! It was awesome.

-- Near-Death-Like Experiencer Mary Deioma

70

Dad went on, and eventually, he came to a huge wigwam, which was glowing with almost fluorescent light. There was a man in the middle of the wigwam. He had long white hair and His hair touched the floor. At first, Dad thought the man was dressed all in white. Then he realized that the man was glowing, He was the source of the luminescent light. Dad knelt down in front of Him with a sudden knowledge that this was The Creator. Dad was delighted to see Him.

"Ni Gi iPii Dagoshin," Dad said. "I have arrived."

"Geyaabi. Gii Zhii Du Whin. Wii Doo Ko Daadiwin Gi JI Anishiinabeg." "Go back, child, it's not your time. You're not finished yet. You have to help the people."

-- Dianna Good Sky describing the near-death-like encounter her father, Gene Goodsky, had with The Creator

71

He looked down at me and he said, "you're not supposed to be here. It's not time for you to be here."

And I remember looking up at him and saying, "but I want to be here." With all my heart, I wanted to be there. I wanted to go Home. I was happy.

And he took a pause and you could see him thinking about something and deciding whether to say something. And with that . . . there was a picture placed in my head of a memory of my original agreement of why I had come to Earth to begin with. It was like I remembered and I went, "Oh, right. Right..."

-- Near-Death Experiencer Anne Horn

72

I said, "No way I'm going back. No way. I'm here and I'm going to stay!"

And they said, "No you can't stay."

And I said, "You're not going to send me back."

And then they got me on the one thing that they could have got me on. They said, "You have not fulfilled your duties and responsibilities. You have not fulfilled your karmic duty."

I'm the kind of a guy that when I give my word on something, it's sacred to me. And I knew, as I thought about it, yes, there were still certain things that I had promised to do when I was a child to help make this a better world, societal service, and I said, "OK, I'll go back."

With that, I felt myself being raised up again, turned around, [and sent back] into the tunnel...

-- Unidentified Near-Death Experiencer #1

73

There were beings, not that I could see, but that I was aware of. They were compassionate, loving, incredibly caring beings. They said this is the entrance to the next level of life . . . These are some of our concepts. If you feel that you can contribute to them, or even understand them, you are welcome to come in . . . They actually gave me all the experiences of all my lifetimes to make the decision whether to come in. I looked at these concepts and frankly, I didn't understand them. I thought I just didn't know enough. And I communicated to these amazing beings, "I think I ought to go back." And then I was aware for the first time of the huge humor that's in the universe; of the sort of chuckle of appreciation. And the voices in unison said, "We think you should."

-- Near-Death Experiencer Harnish Miller

-Three-
Life Reviews: Loving, Learning, The Little Things

Life Reviews are one of the most dramatic and transformative aspects of near-death experiences. They reveal, in microscopic detail, every aspect of our earthly lives. This includes the way our thoughts and actions affected others, including plants and animals. What is perhaps most remarkable about Life Reviews is the surprising emphasis they place on the small, seemingly insignificant events of our lives...

74

Although my near-death experience was nearly 34 years ago, there is virtually not a day that goes by that I am not aware of making decisions based on that experience.

-- Near-Death Experiencer Geraldine Berkheimer

75

I keep a first-grade picture of myself at my bedside to remind me every morning that I am a child of God. When I am faced with a difficult situation or someone makes me mad, I stop a second to decide what I am going to do. I know I'm going to have to do another Life Review and I do not want to review it in a hurtful way again. I'm not perfect, but I really try hard to do the right thing. Besides that, I know He is watching me.

-- Near-Death-Like Experiencer Mary W

76

The Life Review is one of the best teaching tools for spiritual development because we actually see and feel exactly how our choices, actions, and inaction impacted others and the greater world during our lifetime.

-- Near-Death Experience Researcher Jeff Janssen

77

The near-death experience isn't given just to those who have the experience, it's given to all of us to learn from, because all of us can profit from the lessons near-death experiencers learn in the course of a Life Review or other aspects of their experience.

We can grow from these lessons. We can apply these lessons into our daily lives.

-- Near-Death Experience Researcher Kenneth Ring, PhD

78

The Golden Rule is not just a precept for moral conduct -- it's the way it works! And you experience this during the Life Review. You learn that lesson in a very forceable way as a result of going through this kind of experience. And that's why, when people have NDEs, they change as much as they do! If you can even imagine what it must be like to go through your entire life and see everything you've ever done, without judgment, but from a kind of almost omniscient point of view with regard to the effects of those actions, and you see what your actions do to other people, it's a heavy kind of lesson. It's something that stays with you and informs your conduct . . . after your near-death experience.

-- Near-Death Experience Researcher Kenneth Ring, PhD

79

I have a friend who when growing up was kind of a roughneck; he had a hot temper; he was always getting into scrapes. One day he was driving his truck through the suburb in the town where he lived and he almost hit a pedestrian. And he got very aggravated with the pedestrian. He was a very big physical guy and a fight ensued. He punched this guy out and left him unconscious on the pavement, got back into his truck, and roared off.

15 years later my friend has a near-death experience . . . and during the near-death experience, he has a Life Review. In his Life Review, this particular scene of the fight takes place again. And he said that, as many people do, he experienced this from a dual aspect. There was a part of him that was almost as if he were high up in a building looking out a window and seeing the fight below. But at the same time, he was observing the fight like a spectator, he saw himself in the fight. Except this time, he found himself in the role of the other person. And he felt all 32 blows that he had rained on this person 15 years ago now being inflicted upon himself. He felt his teeth cracking. He felt the blood in his teeth. He felt everything that this other person must have felt at that particular time. There was a complete role reversal; an empathic Life Review experience.

-- Near-Death Experience Researcher Kenneth Ring, PhD

80

From the time I stepped out of the truck, I hit that man 32 times. I saw what an enraged Tom Sawyer not only looked like but felt like. I experienced seeing Tom Sawyer's fist come directly into my face. I felt my teeth going through my lower lip.

In other words, I was in that man's eyes. I was in that man's body. I experienced the physical pain, the degradation, the embarrassment, the humiliation, and the helplessness in being knocked back like that. I broke his nose and really made a mess of his face. I almost killed that man. He didn't have time to bring his hands up, he fell straight backwards hitting his head on the street...

In the Life Review, I came to know the man's chronological age: he was 46 years old. I knew that he was in a drunken state and that the rationale behind his desire to drink to oblivion was that he was in a severe state of bereavement for his deceased wife. He turned to alcohol as an escape mechanism for dealing with her death. I experienced unbelievable things about that man that are of a very personal, confidential, and private nature.

-- Near-Death Experiencer Tom Sawyer

81

When you die, everything you have said, thought, or done will be known by all. There are no secrets in the afterlife.

-- Near-Death Experiencer Sandra Rogers

82

The most important of my actions was an instant I would never have recalled except for the near-death experience . . . I had taken a child aside on a very hot day. And this was not a charming or a particularly lovable child. But I wanted this child to feel loved; I wanted this child to feel, really, the love of God that brought him into existence and that brought us all into existence . . . I took him aside and gave him something to drink and just spent some time with him . . . And that was the greatest of all actions. That filled with me with unspeakable and incomprehensible joy. And it was not an action that anyone noticed. And it was not an action that I even recalled. And it was not an action that I had done with any thought of reward. It was simply an action motivated by love. By selfless love.

-- Near-Death Experiencer Reinee Pasarow

83

I experienced in a holographic awareness that was instantaneous, how every action that one takes is like a stone cast in the water . . . A purely loving action was the most wonderful thing that I could ever have achieved in my life. This had more meaning than to have been a Rockefeller, or president of the United States, or to have been a great scientist, and to have invented something incredible. If I had committed a truly pure and loving action, it reverberated throughout the stuff of every individual on the planet, and I felt that action reverberating through them and through myself.

-- Near-Death Experiencer Reinee Pasarow

84

The Life Review continued all the way down to third grade. I was teasing a smaller girl . . . calling her names . . . she's standing against the wall crying . . . And now I'm on the receiving end, meaning I'm her . . . And not only am I feeling her sorrow and her pain, but I'm seeing, sensing, and feeling the pain and sorrow in her parents because she's now going to turn out as a shyer and more inward person . . . I am also feeling how my actions caused ripples far away, not just in her life, but in her parents' lives, in her whole family, also in everyone around her. So, I really get a full spectrum of the full consequences -- all the links in the chain -- to spending a few minutes in a schoolyard teasing a girl.

-- Near-Death-Like Experiencer Rene Jorgensen

85

EVERYTHING I ever thought, did, said, hated, helped, did not help, should have helped, was shown in front of me . . . like a movie. How mean I'd been to people, how I could have helped them, how mean I was (unintentionally also) to animals! Yes!

Even the animals had feelings. It was horrible. I fell on my face in shame. I saw how my acting, or not acting, rippled in effect towards other people and their lives. It wasn't until then that I understood how each little decision or choice affects the world. The sense of letting my Savior down was too real. Strangely, even during this horror, I felt a compassion, an acceptance of my limitations by Jesus and the crowd of others.

-- Near-Death Experiencer Alexa H

86

The information was flowing at an incredible speed that probably would have burned me up if it hadn't been for the extraordinary Energy holding me ... God interjected love into everything, every feeling, every bit of information about absolutely everything that went on, so that everything was all right. There was no good and no bad. There was only me -- and my loved ones from this life -- trying to survive ... just trying to be. I realize now that without God holding me, I would not have had the strength to experience what I did.

-- Near-Death Experiencer Barbara Harris Whitfield

87

The Light is so warm and so glowing and so forgiving. The Light has no judgement. There was no condemnation. There was no blaming. No shame. There was nothing but love and acceptance. The Light knew everything I had ever thought, done, or will do.

-- Near-Death Experiencer Andy Petro

88

Entirety does not describe the fullness of this review. It included knowledge about me, that all the books in the world couldn't contain. I understood every reason for everything I did in my life. And I also understood the impact I had on others. A part of me began to anticipate certain events, things in my life I would dread seeing again. But most of them didn't show up, and I understood that I had taken responsibility for these actions and had repented them. I saw myself repenting for them, sincerely wanting God to remove the weight and guilt of those terrible actions. And He had. I marveled at His sublime love and that my misdeeds could be forgiven and removed so easily. But then I saw other scenes that I hadn't anticipated, things that were just as awful. I saw them in horrible detail and watched the impact they had on others. I saw that I had let many people down in my life. I had made commitments to friends and family that I had just let things ride until they were irreversibly unfulfilled. People had depended on me, and I had said, I'm too busy or it's not my problem, and just let it go. My cavalier attitude had caused real pain and heartache in others, pain I had never known about.

-- Near-Death Experiencer RaNelle Wallace

89

I re-experienced myself doing good things, but they were fewer and less significant than I had thought. Most of the great things I thought I had done were almost irrelevant. I had done them for myself. I had served people when it served me to do so. I had founded my charity on conditions of repayment, even if the repayment was merely a stroke to my ego. Some people had been helped, however, by my small acts of kindness, a smile, a kind word, little things I had long since forgotten. I saw that people were happier because of my actions and in turn were kinder to others. I saw that I had sent out waves of goodness and hope and love when I had only meant to smile or to help in a small way. But I was disappointed at how few of these incidents there were. I had not helped as many people as I thought.

-- Near-Death Experiencer RaNelle Wallace

90

My angel showed me a second vision, a scene I'd forgotten. I now saw myself at 17, when I'd worked at a convalescent hospital after school. I had grown fond of a toothless old woman who was no longer able to speak clearly, and who never had visitors. She liked to suck on graham crackers before going to bed, but no one wanted to serve her because when she had finished, she would drool as she kissed the entire length of the arm of the person feeding her. While others avoided her, I willingly fed her the cookies she adored, seeing how happy this made her. When that scene was replayed for me, I felt as if every loving spirit in God's kingdom was thanking me in unison. I was amazed that such an act could have meant so much to God -- and to me. I felt humbled and very honored.

-- Near-Death Experiencer Dianne Morrissey

91

I went to fill up the bucket but, on my way back, I felt that the bucket was way too heavy for me. I decided to empty some of the water to make the bucket lighter. Instead of emptying the water right there, I noticed a tree that was alone by itself in a dry patch of land. I took the effort to go out of my way to that tree and emptied some of the water at the tree base. I even waited there a few seconds to make sure the water is soaked in the soil and is absorbed. In my Life Review, I received such an applaud and joy for this simple act that it is unbelievable. It was like all the spirits in the universe were filled with joy from this simple act and were telling me, "We are proud of you." That simple act seemed to be one of the best things I had ever done in my life! This was strange to me, because I didn't think this little act was a big deal and thought I had done much more important and bigger things. However, it was shown to me that what I had done was extremely valuable because I had done it purely from the heart, with absolutely no expectation for my own gain.

-- Near-Death Experiencer Mohammad Z

92

I was a 10-year-old boy. I had bullied and mercilessly beaten another boy who was also around my age. He felt tortured and deeply hurt. In my Life Review, I saw that scene again. The boy was crying in physical and deep emotional pain. As he was walking in the street crying and going back home, he radiated negative energy which affected everything around him and on the path. People, and even birds, trees, and flies, received this negative energy from him, which kept propagating throughout the universe. Even rocks on the side of the street were affected by his pain. I saw that everything is alive and our way of grouping things in categories of "alive" and "not alive" is only from our limited physical point of view. In reality, everything is alive . . . When this boy went home to his parents, I saw the impact that seeing him in that state had on his parents. I felt the feeling and pain it created in them and how it affected their behavior from that point forward. I saw that as a result of this action, his parents would be always more worried when their son was away from home or if he was a few minutes late.

-- Near-Death Experiencer Mohammad Z

93

Berkley Carter Mills relived each incident in his life, including killing a mother bird when he was eight. He was so proud of that single shot until he felt the pain the bird's three babies went through when they starved to death without her.

-- Near-Death Experiencer and Researcher P.M.H. Atwater

94

Kimberly Clark Sharp once shared an interesting near-death account of the Life Review of a woman who saw an event in her life as a child. The lesson the woman learned from her Life Review is that our actions which seem unimportant can be more important than we can imagine on the other side. When the woman was a little girl, she saw a tiny flower growing almost impossibly out of a crack in the sidewalk. She bent down and cupped the flower and gave it her full unconditional love and attention. When the girl became a woman and had an NDE, during her Life Review she discovered that it was this incident with the flower that was the most important event of her entire life. The reason was because it was the moment where she expressed her love in a greater, purer, and unconditional manner.

-- Near-Death Experience Researcher Kevin Williams

95

I loved the appearance of a tree. In my Life Review I could experience a bit of what the tree experienced in my loving it, two little photons of love and adoration. It was somewhat like the leaves acknowledging my presence. Can a tree experience that? Yes, it can. Don't go kicking trees anymore! You do have that effect on plants. You do have an effect on animals. You do have an effect on the universe. And in your Life Review you'll be the universe and experience yourself in what you call your lifetime and how it affects the universe. In your Life Review you'll be yourself absolutely, in every aspect of time, in every event, in the over-all scheme of things in your lifetime.

-- Near-Death Experiencer Tom Sawyer

96

"Kindness is God's love in action."

-- What The Light told Near-Death Experiencer Shekina Rose

97

I saw myself at five years old. It was with my brothers and sisters and my neighborhood friend named Heidi... He picked up a stick and whacked a beehive and we all took off and ran. Everyone got into the public building, but the last one was Heidi. And I had a devious thought. I said, "I'm going to hold the door and not let Heidi in and see what happens to Heidi." All those bees from that beehive, they stung the daylights out of Heidi. And every single bee sting I felt. I felt every sting. The burning sensation. The swelling. His mother came to the public building scared and frightened. I felt all her fear. All her fright. All her rage. His father came out there trying to figure out what [happened]. I felt it all. It rippled. I felt every single thing.

-- Near-Death Experiencer Roland Webb

98

My niece once asked me, "What have near-death experiences taught you that that you didn't already know; that you didn't learn from studying other spiritual paths?"

My answer was, "I learned two things from near-death experiences that I didn't learn from other sources. The first was how all the puzzle pieces of life fit together. The second was the special emphasis that NDEs give to certain aspects of life. One example is the importance that NDEs place on ordinary, everyday, seemingly insignificant interactions. Turns out the way we treat the cashier, the neighbor's dog, the tree in our front yard can reverberate across the universe."

-- Near-Death Experience Researcher David Sunfellow

99

At the end of it, no one is going to judge you but yourself. You will be accountable for everything you've done here. But not accountable like you are going to be punished. It is not going to happen like that. You are going to be accountable because you will understand and see what you did and what you should have done. And you, from the love of who you are; the immense love that you are, you will want to do something about it, and you will not allow it to not be corrected and fixed by yourself.

-- Near-Death Experiencer Julie Aubier

100

Consider the story of a former Nazi who hurt people in big ways, by killing them in concentration camps. He had an NDE while he was in a coma. The coma lasted forty-eight hours, but it seemed to him that it lasted a lifetime. He was in a dark cave with Nazi and Roman soldiers who had been responsible for mass killings. After a while, he saw a different part of the place where light was shining, and there were the people he had killed. He wanted to ask their forgiveness. He heard that he had already been forgiven, and that now he only needed to forgive himself. He felt unable do this, and so he was allowed to feel the pain and suffering he had caused each of his victims. Afterward, all these people comforted him. "He was bathed in unconditional love; it permeated his entire being." Then he awoke from his coma.

-- Near-Death Experience Researchers Sheila, Dennis, and Matthew Linn

101

This recounting for the deeds of one's life is not what you would think at all in terms of this life. Because what was important were the choices I made. And what was more important than the choices I made, were my motivations and my intent, and really the state of my heart in doing any single action.

-- Near-Death Experiencer Reinee Pasarow

102

Many events in my life I experienced not from how I remembered it, but from the point of view of how people, animals, and the environment experienced it around me. I felt it as my own. The times I had made others happy, or sad, I felt it all as they did. It was very apparent that every single thought, word, and action affects everything around us and indeed the entire universe. Trees, plants, animals too. I have been a long-term vegetarian since about 18 years old and I know this was appreciated and is a good choice in life. Spiritually, it seemed to show proof of respect for all life, and even seemed to balance some of the negative and wicked things I have done in my life.

-- Near-Death Experiencer Justin U

103

In this other realm, my uncle and I were suddenly merged together . . . I became aware of things that I could not have known about my uncle in this world. I discovered that he was a person of tremendous courage, though to look at him in this life, you might not know it. Although he was a tall, impressive, stoic-looking individual with classic Native American features, he was also a quiet, reserved, and very humble man. During this reunion, I learned that he was someone who would stand up for things that he truly believed in and that he had struggled with and had overcome some huge challenges in his life. I had never heard him spoken of as a heroic type; however, I learned through this encounter that this courage was almost unspeakably great in him.

-- Near-Death Experiencer Reinee Pasarow

104

I came to realize that the people who were most important were often the ones who we might consider to be the least important in this world. I learned to see people very differently, in a new light. To give one example: consider someone who has fought hard to overcome addiction. Such a person might not be looked upon favorably in this physical world for having had an addiction. However, the tremendous struggle, the strength, and the courage that it took to overcome the powerful hold of addiction, is viewed as quite admirable in the next world. Here, we often judge people negatively for the challenges which they face, rather than by the character, fortitude, and courage they develop from facing and overcoming those immense challenges.

-- Near-Death Experiencer Reinee Pasarow

105

Even though I had been an atheist for years, I felt God's love. This love was holding me. It felt incredible. There are no words in the English language, or maybe in this reality, to explain the kind of love God emanates. God was totally accepting of everything we -- God and I -- reviewed in my life.

-- Near-Death Experiencer Barbara Harris Whitfield

106

In the Life Review we judge ourselves; no one else does. The Light/God did not. But with no ego left -- and no lies -- we can't hide from what we have done and feel remorse and shame, especially in the presence of this love and light. Some of the things in life we think of as important don't seem to be so important there. But some of the insignificant things from the material human perspective are very important spiritually.

-- Near-Death Experiencer Justin U

107

I was shown it is not the big things we do in life that make the difference. All the little things we do each day make the difference. Little acts of kindness mean so much to God.

-- Near-Death-Like Experiencer Mary W

108

As the Being of Light moved away . . . I had gained the knowledge that I could use to correct my life. I could hear the Being's message in my head:

"Humans are powerful spiritual beings meant to create good on the Earth. This good isn't usually accomplished in bold actions, but in singular acts of kindness between people. It's the little things that count, because they are more spontaneous and show who you truly are."

-- Near-Death Experiencer Dannion Brinkley

109

One of the greatest light-bulb moments during my experience occurred when I learned "the smallest acts of kindness were immense acts," spiritually speaking. Why? Simply because the ego is not involved in those acts. We do them simply because we are motivated by our inner voice to do them. It is the loving thing to do! We do not expect a pat on the back, or any type of reciprocity for doing the small act. In fact, we don't even think we are doing any great significance when we do it. This is a HUGE, HUGE spiritual deed and something my Great Teacher, the Light of God, wanted me to help people realize. Because when we unselfishly do this, we are expressing through us The Light into the world. THE LIGHT!!! Every day there are countless ways of elevating ourselves to a higher and more Divine Light-embodied soul-being simply by responding to the love within us through doing small acts of kindness.

-- Near-Death Experiencer Nancy Clark

110

I thought [loving other people] was going to be easy, but it turns out to be the hardest thing I've ever done . . . It's easy for me to love my mother because she was a really nice woman; a very loving woman. It's not hard to love someone who is really good and really loving. But what do you do with someone who is difficult, or really nasty? Those are hard people to love. And what does it mean to love someone? Sometimes to love someone means you need to incarcerate them. And that's not a lot of fun. Sometimes loving someone means you have to put as much distance between them and you as possible and tell them to never call you. And that's not a lot of fun. Loving people sounds so simple, but it's very difficult.

-- Near-Death Experiencer Howard Storm

111

I asked God, "How do I know right from wrong?"

He replied, "Right is helping and being kind. Wrong is not only hurting someone but not helping when you can."

-- Near-Death Experiencer Cecil (age 11)

112

When you waved a loving goodbye to a good friend the other day, did you affect the clouds up above? Did you actually affect them? Do a butterfly's wings in China affect the weather here? You better believe they do. You can learn all of that in a Life Review!

-- Near-Death Experiencer Tom Sawyer

113

I learned that everything we do matters. Even the person you smile to on your way to the bakery or work. Even the creatures big and small that you bend over to pet. Nothing goes unnoticed. It all matters. My purpose is to stand up for the meek, to be compassionate, but most of all, to love.

-- Near-Death Experiencer Melinda G

114

I'm not asking you to believe anything. I'm simply telling you what I believe. And I have no idea what the next life will be like. Whatever I saw was only from the doorway, so to speak. But it was enough to convince me totally of two things from that moment on: One, that our consciousness does not cease with physical death; that it becomes, in fact, keener and more aware than ever. And secondly, that how we spend our time on Earth, the kind of relationships we build, is vastly more important than we can know.

-- Near-Death Experiencer George Ritchie, MD

115

I have never interviewed anyone who had a near-death experience who told me that they came back to make more money or to spend more time at their jobs away from their families . . . Instead, they become convinced that they need to be more loving, and kind. They react to their experience by living life to its fullest. They believe their lives have a purpose, even if that purpose is obscure to them. Invariably it involves concepts such as love of family or service to others. They seem to know that the love they create while living will be reflected and radiated back to them when they die.

-- Near-Death Experience Researcher Melvin Morse, MD

116

For me personally, I'm showing more love to others now than before I started my near-death-experience studies. My understanding of near-death experiences has made me a better doctor. I face life with more courage and confidence. I believe

NDErs really do bring back a piece of the afterlife. When NDErs share their remarkable experiences, I believe a piece of the afterlife, in some mysterious way, becomes available to us all.

-- Near-Death Experience Researcher Jeffrey Long, MD

117

My near-death experience was the event in my life that has brought about the most significant change deep inside me. I came out of this accident severely disabled having lost one leg and one arm, but the deepest sense of this near-death experience was of greater importance to me. The meaning of my NDE was not how successful I was or which managerial values I have created, but the only thing that was important was what kind of person I was. My thesis is that all people who have a near-death experience feel the same way . . . Based on the knowledge I gained from this experience, I had to alter my way of life and set the priorities differently. Before the accident, the highest priority for me was to advance enterprise developments, work, and success. After the accident, my first priority were my family and my children. Business and financial issues came second.

-- Near-Death Experiencer Joachim Schoss

118

We run after values that, at death, become zero. At the end of your life, nobody asks you how many degrees you have, or how many mansions you built, or how many Rolls Royces you could afford. That's what dying patients teach you.

-- Near-Death Experience Researcher Elisabeth Kubler-Ross

119

God's not particularly interested in our material success in this world, but He's interested in our relationships -- how much we love one another -- that's what God cares about. And if you are doing your very best, no matter how humble it is, to love one another, God is EXTREMELY PLEASED with what you are doing.

-- Near-Death Experiencer Howard Storm

120

You are loved and the reason you are here is to love others; you are loved and your mission here is to help people remember that they are love.

-- Near-Death Experiencer Chris Batts

121

The point of all of this was for me is to bring heaven into my own life and the lives of the people around me. And to anybody else who wanted to listen.

-- Near-Death Experiencer Nancy Rynes

122

After your death, when most of you for the first time realize what life here is all about, you will begin to see that your life here is almost nothing but the sum total of every choice you have made during every moment of your life. Your thoughts, which you are responsible for, are as real as your deeds. You will begin to realize that every word and every deed affects your life and has also touched thousands of lives.

-- Near-Death Experience Researcher Elisabeth Kubler-Ross

123

God reminded me that the only thing I would get to bring back with me was love; the love I gave away.

-- Near-Death Experiencer Laura M

124

Ever since the experience, I have carried a terrific sense of urgency to share it with the lonely, discouraged and dis-eased people such as alcoholics, drug addicts, and the social outcast. I have shared what I have learned with my patients and audiences, the knowledge that a God of love loves us regardless of our race, creed, or color. I have received many letters and have had patients say that sharing my experiences with them has either saved them from committing suicide or completely turned their lives around because it gave them a much better understanding of God's love and plan for their lives.

-- Near-Death Experiencer George Ritchie, MD

125

I came to sell you something. Yes, I'm a salesperson. I came to sell you life insurance. But not the type of life insurance in this world; life insurance for the other world.

When you leave this world, you're not taking nothing with you -- nothing but your good deeds. You're not taking money; you're not taking nothing. You can only take your good deeds and the Torah that you studied. That's it.

When you are standing in front of those judges, everything is just weight. Sometimes a small deed is worth so much. Some small deed that you do in this world can change completely how you are being judged. There are so many little things that you can just do. Just give a smile to another person, be nicer to your wife, be nicer to your kids, be nicer to another person. Be honest.

-- Near-Death Experiencer Alon Anava

126

It's only when we truly know and understand that we have a limited time on Earth -- and that we have no way of knowing when our time is up, we will then begin to live each day to the fullest, as if it was the only one we had.

-- Near-Death Experience Researcher Elisabeth Kubler-Ross

127

Before you go to bed tonight, try to imagine that you don't know whether you will wake up tomorrow. It would be your last day. Or as far as I'm concerned, you've got two more days. What would you do with them? Would you spend the next day the same way as the last one hundred? Or would you change something?

-- Near-Death Experiencer Joachim Schoss

128

A simple act of kindness, like a ripple on a pond, radiates from the giver throughout eternity.

-- Near-Death Experiencer Sandra Rogers

129

"RaNelle," Grandmother said, "there is one more thing I need to say to you. Tell everybody that the key is love."

"The key is love," she repeated.

"The key is love," she said a third time.

Then she let go of my hand, and the word "love" reverberated in my mind as I left her and fell into a deep blackness. I was crying as I left the world of light and glory and love.

-- Near-Death Experiencer RaNelle Wallace

130

I asked God, "Is there anything you want me to tell these people when I go back to Earth?"

"Go and tell everyone that I love them."

"That's it?"

"That's it."

-- Near-Death Experiencer Chris Batts

131

I asked Jesus this question, "Why am I so depressed all of the time?"

Jesus answered, "You forgot that I love you."

-- Near-Death-Like Experiencer Krystal Winzer

132

"Don't waste your life thinking you're not loved."

-- What Jesus told Near-Death Experiencer Yolaine Stout

133

God's Final Exam questions have nothing to do with the amount of money in our bank account, the size of our house, or how many awards we might have won. NDErs tell us the value and significance of our time on Earth all comes down to one thing: how well have we loved. Ultimately, God wants and challenges us to be love, give love, and receive love in everything we do. Earth is then indeed a spiritual development school where we experientially learn how to more fully and unconditionally love ourselves and others. It is our primary purpose in coming here and, in the end, we judge and grade ourselves on how well we have truly learned to give and receive love.

-- Near-Death Experience Researcher Jeff Janssen

134

"What have you done with your life?"

-- What Jesus asked Near-Death Experiencer George Ritchie

135

"In life, what did you do with what you had?"

-- What The Light asked Near-Death Experiencer Joyce H. Brown

136

"What good have you done?"

-- What a Divine Power asked Near-Death Experiencer Robert Bare

137

"What did you do for your fellow man?"

-- What Jesus asked Near-Death Experiencer Chris Markey

138

"How did you love? What did you do to help others?"

-- What a spiritual being asked Near-Death Experiencer Nicole Dron

139

"To what degree have you learned to love?"

-- What a Divine Energy asked Near-Death Experiencer Jeff Olsen

-Four-
Lighten Up; Don't Take Life So Seriously

Another hallmark of near-death experiences is their insistence that life is beautiful, purposeful, and fun. God, it turns out, laughs. God has a sense of humor. God is cheerful and lighthearted. We should be, too. Lightening up and not taking things so seriously is one of the best ways to ease our earthly burdens and lift the earthly burdens of others...

140

The Light has a fantastic sense of humor! We reviewed some of the really silly things that I did in my lifetime and we would be laughing at how serious I took them. Because life down here is an illusion. It's a game. Don't take it so seriously. The Light has a wonderful sense of humor.

-- Near-Death Experiencer Andy Petro

141

I became aware that the God I was experiencing was not just a life force, or some impersonal consciousness, but God had a personality, an integrity like the father I had never known. God had a sense of humor! He and I both laughed at the thought of me questioning His existence. It seemed to me the absolutely funniest thought in the world, and we laughed at the thought of it. I realized that I was the shadow, and He was the reality. The very idea that I would question His existence was a source of laughter for God and me. I was sobbing, overcome by the sheer amount of love that swept through me and over me, and laughing at the same time.

-- Near-Death Experiencer John K

142

It seemed impossible that I could be loved and accepted just as I was in that moment. Released from the burden of self-punishment, embraced in the wholeness of this forgiving Presence, I was enveloped in joy. I seemed to become transparent, the light of divine love flowing through me. Then I heard . . . soft, benevolent laughter, which felt like the wise and gentle smile of the Buddha. Again, I was surprised and perplexed; I had not expected to hear laughter from a divine force. It rained over me like soft petals. Then It said: "My child, you mustn't take things so seriously. You are just part of an evolutionary chain, in which all life evolves at different stages of development. You are only human. You need not judge yourself so harshly. Be gentle with yourself." I had gotten only the slightest glimpse of the limitless realms beyond the finite boundaries of the world we inhabit. I was eager to learn more.

-- Near-Death Experiencer Lee Thornton

143

This glorious, wonderful Entity recognized me, understood perfectly every minute aspect about me, and poured love into me. The love was real, as much a force as a feeling, and immeasurable. Knowing every little thing about me and my life and viewing it along with me, there was a lot of real amusement. This Being has a personality. It is fun to be with, delightful, and it has a sense of humor. I never wanted to leave this Divine Presence, but somehow, without explanation, but with perfect understanding, I knew that I had to go back, and I understood that this was good and right.

-- Near-Death Experiencer Brian T

144

He reminded me that it was not my time and that I needed to return to my body and resume my earth life. I reminded Him that He had promised me free agency, and I was choosing to exercise that agency to stay with Him. He laughed with great joy and mirth at my stubbornness, saying, "Yes, Laura, I would expect you to argue for your own case. The decision will of course be yours! But first let me show you some things."

I was suddenly struck with wonderment and awe. He knew me. Everything about me was already known. I was part of His creation and in me was the spark of God; it could not be otherwise. He was all knowing, He was all love, and I was a part of it all.

-- Near-Death Experiencer Laura M

145

God called me by name and told me I could not stay. I protested. I told Him all of my services on Earth -- working 24/7, not much money for my work, a good wife, a good mother. I did not want to leave this place.

Then God said, "Let me ask you one question. Have you ever loved another person the way you have been loved here?"

The love I had received in there was so overpowering. I had never felt anything like it, so I answered God honestly. I said, "No, it is impossible. I am just a human. You are God."

He gave me the illusion of a sweet protective chuckle. He then said, "Mary, you can do better."

-- Near-Death Experiencer Mary Jo Rapini

146

I was about to cross this stream, when all of a sudden, I was engulfed with a beautiful, warm and bright light, which somehow felt like a cloud. I felt arms around me, and The Light talked with me. It told me that I would not be able to stay; that I had much work left to do and I had to go back to finish it. I am a very stubborn person, so I began to argue with The Light telling it that I was not going back. I even stomped my foot (however, I don't think I had a foot or anything like that; it was more like I was floating). I have always said after this experience that God has a beautiful sense to humor, because when I stomped my foot and said I did not want to go back and I was NOT going back, there was this little chuckle and The Light smiled at me and said, "Oh, yes you will" and of course I did come back.

-- Near-Death Experiencer Florence W

147

Jesus laughed and then gave me the answer, not in words but in a "knowing" that encompassed not just the element of the question, but a complete understanding of all relational aspects of the question. He has a wonderful sense of humor, and I distinctly got the feeling that He enjoys us humans as a father enjoys watching the minor scrapes children get themselves into.

-- Near-Death Experiencer Terry E

148

I was aware that Light knew me better than I knew myself. Despite any of my foibles, eccentricities, poor decisions, and plain old humanness, It loved me to the core. It found the seriousness with which I viewed myself amusing. It seemed to be certain that in the end, all of my problems, hurts, inflicted hurts, and my life in general would be redemptive in the sense that it would ultimately end in love.

-- Near-Death Experiencer Jo B

149

I remember after my experience I had the simplest situation where two cable guys showed up at my house . . . What I discovered was the Divine having a sense of humor. Things are funny. The two cable guys show up at the house and they were wearing their uniforms for work and they were there to hook up the cable for the TV. My husband had made an appointment and he had to go to work right after my NDE. [He] was very busy taking care of the family, and so I was at home in this state with kids just trying to figure out how to function. And the cable guys show up and when I opened the door, I saw them how the Divine sees them and I couldn't stop laughing. I was trying not to be rude but to me they looked like -- if you imagine little kids going into the closet and trying clothes on and trying to look really serious and showing up at the door and be like "We're the cable guys." I can't describe it. I was like "Oh, OK." I brought them in, and they were just really serious about their job like, "We're here to hook up the TV." To me it was just so funny because I was so disconnected from things like watching TV, and watching football, or sitcoms . . . I just didn't realize that this appointment was coming and while they were hooking it up, they were asking me really simple questions like "OK, so what channel do you want? Do you want ESPN? Do you want the cartoon channel?" Everything they were asking me was busting me up.

I got to where I felt like I was being rude, because they have an important job. There's nothing that isn't important. Everything that people do is part of their own vital experience, and it's all beautiful really. It's just that it felt totally different to me. I had to actually -- I told them I'm really sorry; I think I'm sick or something. And one of the guys said, "Did you take some NyQuil?" And I was wiping the tears and blowing my nose, and I finally said, "You know what, you guys can hook up anything you want, because I need to leave the room." And so, I had to leave, because I knew at some point it was going to look like I was being rude...

I saw people from then on the way we see toddlers when they're playing. I see that despite how we age here -- we get older and we take ourselves seriously and we think, you know, I have this important thing I'm doing -- but the Divine is like: "Lighten up. It's OK, you can lighten up." And I tend to be so serious from what I came from. I worry so much. I thought things were so serious, and I wanted to please God, and I prayed so much, and now through the Divine I was seeing that it's totally OK to just have fun and laugh. I was laughing so much, I was wheezing...

-- Near-Death Experiencer Amy Call

150

Angela Williams: I was in this bliss and it was like I was plugged into the motherboard. I had this expansive experience of everything, just all your senses are super-sized. It was like this infinite divine consciousness that you really don't have any questions. It's like you have this knowing, and that's the only way I can explain it. But then all of a sudden, I heard these words, "You cannot stay."

Lee Witting: Were those the first words you heard on the other side?

Angela Williams: Yes.

Lee Witting: Did you know it was God speaking?

Angela Williams: Oh yes. And I panicked, and I started begging God not to send me back. Then at one point I stopped, and I thought to myself, "Oh my God, I am arguing with God!" I had that self-realization and then God chuckled, and it was almost as if God was like, "Yeah, I've heard that a million times."

Lee Witting: I'm so glad to hear that God has a sense of humor about these things.

-- Near-Death Experiencer Angela Williams being interviewed by Lee Witting on NDE Radio

151

I knew Him, yet I cannot explain how. I just knew Him. He was so alive, so joyful, so free, so mirthful, so playful, and so utterly alive with joy. He radiated joy as if He was the source of all life, joy, truth, goodness, beauty, like a living fountain that continually flowed up, but a living fountain that was its own source of water. This Being had absolutely no condemnation or judgment of anyone or me. It just was not there. I tell you that no one on Earth has ever loved like this Being.

-- IANDS Near-Death Experiencer #5

152

Don't always be so flipping serious. Have fun. Play. Enjoy your life. That's what it is all about. You have a very finite amount of time to come here and enjoy who you are. So, do it.

-- Near-Death Experiencer Nancy Rynes

153

There is no suffering, pain or difficulty, that we can't overcome with a positive thought. I learned that if I laugh at my problems, I laugh with myself, with others, it gives me enormous strength in times of pain.

-- Near-Death Experiencer Ana Cecilia G

154

They assured me that mistakes are an acceptable part of being human. "Go," they said, "and make all the mistakes you want. Mistakes are how you learn." As long as I tried to do what I knew was right, they said, I would be on the right path. If I made a mistake, I should fully recognize it as a mistake, then put it behind me and simply try not to make the same mistake again. The important thing is to try one's best, keep one's standards of goodness and truth, and not to compromise these to win people's approval.

-- Near-Death Experiencer Howard Storm

155

A priest died and went to Heaven. There, he is greeted by a reception committee. After having a whirlwind tour of Heaven, he is told he can enjoy any of Heaven's available recreations.

The priest decided he wanted to read all of the ancient original texts of the Holy Scriptures to understand their true literary meaning. So, he first learned all the languages necessary to accomplish this: Hebrew, Aramaic, Greek and Latin. After becoming a linguistic master, he went to the Heavenly Temple of Knowledge and began to scrutinize the original Biblical texts.

All of a sudden, the priest could be heard crying out loud in the Temple. Angels quickly came to help him, only to find the priest huddled in a corner, crying and muttering to himself, "An 'R'! They left out an 'R'!"

One of the angels comforted the priest and asked him what the problem was. After collecting his wits, the priest sobs again, "It's the letter 'R' ... the word was supposed to be CELEBRATE!"

- Five -
The Purpose Of Life

So why, exactly, are we in this world? Near-death experiences tackle this all-important question from multiple angles. In a nutshell, we are in this world to acquire experiences and abilities that are not available to us in other realms -- and while we are at it, enjoy the ride...

156

True learning happens in the body. This is a big deal to me personally, because so much of my life was about wanting to escape the body and wanting that for other people. I also grew up hearing that when you die you get to take off that glove; you get to be free and so I thought that here [in this world] is the more negative, that there [on the other side of life] is the more positive. The understanding in this place -- as hard as it is to see and understand -- is that true learning happens within the body, because when we are in experience, in this form, there is something that evolves within us at the level of the soul that makes the body an important part of the whole. It isn't that one is good, and one is bad. The two work together in an important way. That was very healing for me personally, to come to a better understanding.

-- Near-Death Experiencer Amy Call

157

One of the main things we came here for was to learn joy. We didn't know what joy was before. When we were up in Heaven, we knew one thing. We knew love. That's what God was. And we learned different concepts, and we learned how to do different things, but we didn't know joy and we wanted to know joy. God told us: "The only way to know joy is to know sorrow." So, we had to come down to this physical realm that He made, so we could learn about sorrow, so we could have joy.

-- Near-Death Experiencer Ryan Rampton

158

We came down here to experience opposition. We came down here to feel the opposite. For example, we would never know what great health felt like if you'd never been sick. You would never know what a wonderful day in Hawaii would be if you didn't live in a winter environment. You'd go to Hawaii in the middle of the winter and you're going, "Yeah, this is awesome!" And the guy on the beach that's local is like, "What's the big deal, man? It's this way every day." So, it's the opposition that defines us. It's the space between things that creates form. All of these things need each other. We need opposition to even know who we are.

-- Near-Death Experiencer Ryan Rampton

159

A lot of spiritual messages seem to be "deny the body, these emotions are bad emotions, these things are not holy" and I don't think that's true. From my experience, everything is holy. Here is there. We didn't come here just to experience all the happy things. We also came here to experience the difficult emotions, because we learn from those and they enrich us in ways that we really can't get when we are out of body, when we are in our Whole Selves. If we could get those out there, we wouldn't be here. From that perspective, it's very exciting to participate in any kind of emotion, and any kind of situation. It's an adventure. It's amazing. It's beautiful . . . It's a kick. It can be really fun.

-- Near-Death Experiencer Natalie Sudman

160

The body is the most magnificent light being there is. The body is a universe of incredible light. Spirit is not pushing us to dissolve this body. That is not what is happening. Stop trying to become God; God is becoming you. Here.

-- Near-Death Experiencer Mellen-Thomas Benedict

161

God gave everything to us, everything is here -- this is where it's at. What we are into now is God's exploration of God through us. People are so busy trying to become God that they ought to realize that we are already God and God is becoming us. That's what it is really about. When I realized this, I was finished with The Void, and wanted to return to this creation.

-- Near-Death Experiencer Mellen-Thomas Benedict

162

The other side is not all it is cracked up to be. There's a lot you can't do on the other side. There's a perfect combination though . . . And we are the perfect matrix of body and spirit. With body and spirit, you can have it all.

-- Near-Death Experiencer Mellen-Thomas Benedict

163

I understood very clearly that being human entitles me to do things that when I am dead, out of my body, I cannot do. Things like drinking a glass of water -- and this is actually my favorite drink since I came back. I love to drink water. It's the most mystical experience I've ever had in my life. The pleasure that I have when I'm drinking a glass of water, with my eyes closed, is just out of this world. So, drinking a glass of water. Eating my favorite food. Feeling the wind on my skin or the rain on my skin. Swimming naked in the river or in the ocean. Hearing birds singing. Having a beautiful kiss. Making love. Even though there are all these different ways of experiencing ecstasy while you are out of your body, the ones that you experience in your flesh are unbelievable.

-- Near-Death Experiencer Julie Aubier

164

Every part of the creation, they explained, is infinitely interesting, because it is a manifestation of the Creator. A very important opportunity for me would be to explore this world with wonder and enjoyment.

-- Near-Death Experiencer Howard Storm

165

Your Higher Self incarnated because as a sensate, embodied being you can have experiences your spirit alone cannot. Don't be afraid of desire. Don't be afraid of passion, of adventure, of a little sin, of failure, of living in your own unique way. Don't be afraid of anything. Life truly is a big play -- have fun with it, don't take it so seriously. Life in all its glory goes on, no matter how messy it looks from here and now.

-- Near-Death Experiencer Cami Renfrow

166

Let it be known that the life that leads to Heaven is not one of withdrawal from the world, but a life in the world, and that a life of piety apart from a life of thoughtfulness (which is possible only in the world) does not lead to Heaven at all. Rather, it is a life of thoughtfulness, a life of behaving honestly and fairly in every duty, every affair, every task, from our deeper nature and therefore from a heavenly source.

-- Near-Death Like Experiencer Emanuel Swedenborg

167

If there is any message I can give, it's not about meditating and leaving your body and taking your Light Being out of this Earth. Indeed, not. It is about bringing The Light into this Earth. Stay here. Be an anchor. Let The Light come in through you into this world. Don't abandon this world. Don't think this place is a bad place and we're going to get out of here. This is a wonderful place. And it's going to get even more wonderful. You are here to anchor The Light, so It can come into this dimension and be here.

-- Near-Death Experiencer Anne Horn

168

The other side does not have the physical pressures that having a body has. Here on Earth, you must feed and clothe that body and provide shelter for it from the elements. You are under continual pressure of some sort, to make decisions that have a spiritual base. You are taught on the other side what you are supposed to do, but can you LIVE it under these pressures on Earth? From what I saw and heard there, it is all about relationships and taking care of each other. Perfection is not expected of people, but learning is expected and considered good progress.

-- Near-Death Experiencer Jean R

169

I was told that the Earth is like a big school, a place where you can apply spiritual lessons learned and test yourself, under pressure, to see if you can actually "live" what you already know you should do.

-- Near-Death Experiencer Jean R

170

"Life's supposed to be hard. You can't skip over parts. You must earn what you receive."

-- What God told Near-Death Experiencer Angie Fenimore, who attempted to end her life via suicide

171

The most beautiful people we have known are those who have known defeat, known suffering, known struggle, known loss, and have found their way out of the depths. These persons have an appreciation, a sensitivity and an understanding of life that fills them with compassions, gentleness, and a deep loving concern. Beautiful people do not just happen.

-- Near-Death Experience Researcher Elisabeth Kubler-Ross

172

I was told to think of my time on Earth as an extended visit to the ultimate theme park. Consider it a place with thrilling rides and various adventures that I could choose to experience or not. I was also reminded that the reason we leave the celestial realm at all was for the excitement, variety, adventure, and entertainment that different incarnations offer.

-- Near-Death Experiencer Duane S

173

It was explained to me how most of our celestial, eternal knowledge is blanked-out during our chosen life spans on Earth. We must temporarily forget most of what our Higher Self already knows, so we can immerse ourselves in the roles we have chosen to play.

-- Near-Death Experiencer Duane S

174

I began getting an information download. There was no talking, just information going into me with absolute love. It was very clear, very loud, and very certain, that WE ARE ALL VERY IMPORTANT TO GOD. We are all deeply, deeply loved by God, and that life is supposed to be hard. It is some sort of proving ground . . . The message was that our lives are deeply important to God and to the existence of the universe. Our love we have and the love we cultivate on Earth, especially for people we have a hard time liking, that love somehow expands the universe and does some very important things.

-- Near-Death Experiencer Heather V

175

It seems like when we create beauty on Earth, it is being manifested in Heaven. When we sing on Earth, it is amplified to the golden ratio in Heaven where it becomes like manna, although in Heaven there is no hunger or thirst.

-- Near-Death Experiencer Heather V

176

A true heart, which is motivated by loving compassion, is what matters in life. Our job is to try to love one another no matter what. It matters very much if we can love or not, because that is our job in this world. We must love! This is what we live for and it doesn't mean we must only love our spouse. It means we need to find out how to love our enemy, because that is why we are here. We are also deeply important to God. Our job on Earth is important. If we don't learn how to love, there are very bad consequences in the multiverse. My sense was strongly that we are needed, and our worth is how much we can love.

-- Near-Death Experiencer Heather V

177

Our job on Earth is to find out how to break through all these illusory walls everywhere that we erect to hide who we are. We need to really love each other and love ourselves. I felt as though there was a sense of humor too. It was like a deep appreciation for our lives and even for our failures. We are supposed to learn from our failures and not beat ourselves up over them.

-- Near-Death Experiencer Heather V

178

All of the people who go through this come away believing that the most important thing in their life is love. For most of them, the second most important thing in life is knowledge. As they see life scenes in which they are learning things, the Being points out that one of the things they can take with them at death is knowledge. The other is love.

-- Near-Death Experience Researcher Raymond Moody, MD

179

God told me there were only two things that we could bring back with us when we died -- LOVE and KNOWLEDGE. So, I was to learn as much about both as possible.

-- Near-Death Experiencer Virginia Rivers

180

I was told that you are here to learn how to love and to gain knowledge. When this was said, not by words but by thoughts, every connotation of the words "love" and "knowledge" were shown to me. I knew it was not just talking about book knowledge or physical love. It meant that I was here on Earth to learn how to accept every race and have no prejudice; that I was to keep expanding and learning about the Earth, nature, animals and people. I felt that this was the mission of all mankind, not just me.

-- Near-Death Experiencer Barbara S

181

One of the prevailing themes that comes out of near-death experiences is that human life has purpose. And that purpose seems to be loving and learning.

-- Near-Death Experience Researcher Janice Holden, EdD

182

I was shown a library filled with gold covered books. These are the lives of people on Earth where their life plan is laid out, and what they hope to achieve through certain key experiences. From what I was shown, people have free choice as to how to get to these preset key experiences. They can take a meandering path of experiences or a more direct route, but there are certain events that are preset and will happen, no matter what. Each of those key events are benchmarks, and their reaction to them will show how much they have learned and what more needs to be done or learned.

-- Near-Death Experiencer Jean R

183

By far the most important lesson coming from the NDE is this: Love is what life is all about. Love is where we all came from. Love is where we will all eventually return. Learning and growing in love is why we are alive . . . The more love one learns and the more love one gives and receives, the better one's life and afterlife will be.

-- Near-Death Experience Researcher Kevin Williams

184

There is only one truly significant work to do in life, and that is love; to love nature, to love people, to love animals, to love creation itself, just because it is. To serve God's creation with a warm and loving hand of generosity and compassion -- that is the only meaningful existence.

-- Near-Death Experiencer George Rodonaia, MD

185

The ultimate lesson all of us have to learn is unconditional love, which includes not only others but ourselves as well.

-- Near-Death Experience Researcher Elisabeth Kubler-Ross

186

I think my mission and everybody's mission is to be here, in three dimensions, in this time, in this space, and to hold the energy of The Light of God. Just hold it . . . If we hold it, we help other people around us find that energy and feel that energy. All you have to remember is there is nothing out there to fear.

You are a divine, powerful being. We all are. We are all part of God. We are all part of love. That's who we are. We are the heart of God. We are here to bring that to planet Earth. To create Heaven on Earth.

-- Near-Death Experiencer Ellyn Dye

187

In my near-death experience, it could not have been more obvious or more simple: Our purpose is to overcome fear, each one of us. We are supposed to utilize faith. We are supposed to let go, let God, trust God. The whole point is LOVE; to remember to choose LOVE instead of fear. It's hard to see these truths while we are wrestling around in the "muck" of life.

-- Near-Death Experiencer Amphianda Baskett

188

When I was in the other realm, where the layers upon layers of my values and beliefs were stripped away, and I was left facing the truth of who I am at my core, I learned that two primary forces -- love and fear -- had been driving all my behaviors. One or the other of these two forces was behind every single action I ever took, and I could clearly see that I had, in fact, spent most of my life being driven by fear, not love. I understood with a sudden stunning clarity that to transform my life, whatever I said or did from that point on would need to come from a place of love instead of fear.

-- Near-Death Experiencer Anita Moorjani

189

My mission, I have come to understand, is to overcome the egoic challenges that all humans face. With humor and humility, we're here to turn fear, anger, selfish greed, and gloating pride into love and compassion for all life.

-- Near-Death Experiencer Louisa Peck

190

God let me ask Him questions. My only question was how could He give me the parents I had? How could he forget all about me and leave me so alone to work my way through those years? What was He thinking?! I have to admit I was pretty angry. He showed me why I had the parents, childhood and life I had experienced. I asked Him for it!!! I chose this life, because I wanted to learn those lessons. Everything was so clear to me -- I had to go through it all to learn what I needed to learn and be able to continue my work here. He never left me alone, and I could see in hindsight that He was always with me.

-- Near-Death-Like Experiencer Mary W

191

No sooner than I'd arrived there that my mother told me I couldn't stay, that I had to go back. That really upset me. I tried pleading with her to let me stay. I told her, "It's my life, I should get to choose. I should have a say-so."

Then she told me, "It's not that you don't get to choose. Part of you, in fact, is choosing and participating in this decision. It would be easy for you to choose to stay here, but you understand on a level you can't quite comprehend just now that there is more from your family relationships you need to experience and learn. And more they need to learn from you. When choosing is not an act of escape but an act of completion, then you will stay."

-- Near-Death Experiencer Naomi

192

There I saw what my life would be, when I come back, between the moment when I come back, and the moment when I finally leave. I would be put on many trials and suffering. I saw myself crying many times. I asked myself: "What have I done to God to deserve all these trials and sufferings?" I was told that before I was born, I had accepted all of this, because through them I would grow. There was some selfish part of me which made me ask: "May I be given in one life what I have to live in other lives on this Earth?" because for me the Earth is a real hell and I did not want to come back. I was told that they could not give me more than my shoulders could carry.

-- Near-Death Experiencer Nicole Dron

193

I was shown how one can never assume that if someone lives a life of suffering that this is because of "evil" deeds. Many may CHOOSE a life of suffering, because of what it awakens in them . . . or to help another, etc. We can NEVER EVER assume that we can be accurate in guessing why each being lives the life they live.

-- Near-Death Experiencer Amy Call

194

I was shown, or could see, my stepmother's whole life -- her struggles, her fears, and all that had made her into who she was. I could finally see her abusiveness was not about me being a "bad" kid. It was ALL because of her fears, her own earthly amnesia, and her struggles, insecurity, etc. I saw that she had been abused growing up. In the end, I could only feel great compassion and even admiration for her that she had been through so much pain, and that she bravely chose her life, knowing it would be confusing and that happiness would be elusive, but that there were important people she needed to touch, and important experiences she needed to have. And I saw that it's pretty much exactly the same for ALL human beings on Earth. We are all blind and scared while we are here. We do our best, and it's all understood, and our mistakes are forgiven once we have our expanded spiritual awareness back.

-- Near-Death Experiencer Amphianda Baskett

195

Not only was I me, I was also my mother, my dad, and my brother. We were all one. Just as I had felt everything my grandmother had felt, I now felt my mother's pain and neglect from her childhood. She wasn't trying to be mean. She didn't know how to be loving or kind. She didn't know how to love. She didn't understand what life is really about. And she was still angry from her own childhood -- angry because they were poor, and because her father was sick almost every day until he died when she was eleven. And then she was angry because he had left her. She didn't know what to do with her anger, so she gave it to my brother and me.

-- Near-Death Experiencer Barbara Harris Whitfield

196

I could see through God's eyes and feel through God's heart. Together, we witnessed how severely I had treated myself because that was the behavior shown and taught to me as a child. I realized that the only big mistake I had made in my 32 years of life was that I had never learned to love myself.

-- Near-Death Experiencer Barbara Harris Whitfield

197

I realized that God wants us to know that we only experience real pain if we die without living first. And the way to live is to give love to ourselves and to others. It seems that we are here to learn to give and receive love. But only when we heal enough to be real can we understand and give and receive love the way love was meant to be.

-- Near-Death Experiencer Barbara Harris Whitfield

198

I felt not only that I was loved unconditionally, it was like I was loved just because I existed -- no other reason. I also felt unconditional love for everyone and everything, even for people that may have hurt me during my life. All I felt for them was unconditional love and compassion and a knowing, that no matter what they did, even if they hurt me really badly . . . they were still doing the best they knew how at the time. It was like I understood why they did what they did.

-- Near-Death Experiencer Anita Moorjani

199

The whole year after my accident was probably one of the hardest years of my life, and I often wondered why I was stupid enough to stay here and not leave when I had the chance. I kept yelling at myself "What the heck were you thinking!?" Now, looking back at what I learned and how blessed I am today, I am so glad I stayed. When I see the rays of sun stream through the clouds sometimes, I get really homesick. To me, God is The Light. That is Him reminding me to remember how much He loves me, and I am never alone. And one day, I'll get to go back to Him. Until then I plan on having a good time. I look at every obstacle as an adventure now, and I'm always looking for the lesson. It's a wonderful game. Life is so much easier this way.

-- Near-Death-Like Experiencer Mary W

200

From the out-of-body perspective, it was understood that it takes some skill to even exist in the physical body, in the physical world. It takes a skill of focus to maintain consciousness within a physical body and then to participate in a collective, cooperative, creative experience of being in this physical world. So, we're all amazing! We're all jet pilots flying 50 feet off the deck upside down. We are very cool. Just by showing up here, just by showing up.

-- Near-Death Experiencer Natalie Sudman

201

We come into this world, at this time, in this place, in order to participate. But that doesn't mean we have to lose sight of the fact of who we really are. We are not this personality, or this body, or these emotions. We are infinite beings having an experience through this body, through the emotions, through the personality. It is possible to participate in this life, to get into a role with passion while still remembering that it is just a role -- that we are actually whole beings: indestructible, safe, utterly beautiful.

-- Near-Death Experiencer Natalie Sudman

202

When we become embodied in the physical, we're learning through our senses, through suffering and joy and all these different levels. We're picking up on so much information . . . , and what we call the Divine is able to receive that information and our learning and our growth -- that's part of why It's intelligent, why It knows. We think It's beyond us; It's so much more intelligent. And yet I understood that It was saying [It was intelligent] because of those willing to go down into the bottom. I understood that Their feeling to us is almost like "You guys are the superheroes who go into the physical body and you experience the suffering. We have nothing but gratitude and love for you."

-- Near-Death Experiencer Amy Call

203

I was with my guide, and I had this enormous gratitude and love . . . I could feel my own humanness wanting to bow to It in a way -- I didn't have the feeling that I needed to bow -- but it's almost like when something is so amazing you just collapse to It, because you love It so much . . . And at the same time, what That is -- what the Divine, what God is -- I felt Its [love and gratitude] coming back to me . . . personally, for exactly who I am, at every level of me, everything I have ever been through, beyond even what I know of in this life time. It was so grateful to me and loved me so much. I felt as if It was bowing to me. So, there was this mutual adoration and love.

-- Near-Death Experiencer Amy Call

500 QUOTES FROM HEAVEN

- Six -
Everything Is Perfect

Of all the mind-bending perspectives that near-death experiences reveal to us, this is the most difficult for humans to understand. How can everything be perfect, when the world we live in is so full of tragedy, injustice, and suffering?

204

I don't recall the exact content of our discussion; in the process of return, the insights that came so clearly and fully in Heaven were not brought back with me to Earth... I do remember this: There was a reason for everything that happened, no matter how awful it appeared in the physical realm. And within myself, as I was given the answer, my own awakening mind now responded in the same manner: "Of course," I would think, "I already know that. How could I ever have forgotten!" Indeed, it appears that all that happens is for a purpose, and that purpose is already known to our eternal self.

-- Near-Death Experiencer Beverly Brodsky

205

I knew with total certainty that everything was evolving exactly the way it should and that the ultimate destiny for every living being is to return to the Source, The Light, Pure Love.

-- Near-Death Experiencer Juliet Nightingale

206

I was allowed to witness all the chaos in the world, but I understood that everything was working according to some greater plan that humans did not comprehend. I understood that even the most horrendous acts had meaning and purpose. Don't ask me to explain this; I can't, because I left the spiritual realm, and I'm now back in the physical realm with all the humanness that living here on this Earth plane encompasses. I, too, have questions -- big questions about suffering and why things happen to good people. But I must say, while I was merged into oneness with the Light of God, I truly did understand that everything makes perfect sense on a spiritual level. EVERY EXPERIENCE WE HAVE IS A STEPPINGSTONE TOWARD OUR GREATEST GOOD AND OUR ULTIMATE SPIRITUAL GROWTH. YES, EVEN TRAGIC EXPERIENCES. That recall helps me to not dwell so much on the answers that would make sense of this suffering, for I know that when I return to that Heavenly Realm, I will once again understand EVERYTHING and why those tragic experiences were needed! Until then, I will be patient and trust in a Higher Power Who loves us through our suffering, Who cries with us, and Who gives us the strength to move through it.

-- Near-Death Experiencer Nancy Clark

207

I wanted to sob with pure joy at the perfection of all creation.

-- Near-Death Experiencer Peggy

208

I was immediately taken up into a wondrous loving presence of light and sound; indescribably wondrous, indescribably loving, beautiful, serene. It was just washing through my being. It was like being a drop of sea water in the ocean. Being part of the ocean, but not being the ocean. Simultaneously, all kinds of things were happening. I had a complete Life Review of my past, present, and future. I was being flooded with this light and sound of all kinds of spiritual principals. I saw the purpose and the function of every religion on the planet. I saw the spiritual purpose and orderliness of war and peace. All of the negativity that we have, has a purpose. I knew what was true of me was true of every other individual also -- that each of us is just indispensable to The Creator. Each of us is like an atom in the body of God.

-- Near-Death Experiencer Tricia Richie

209

In the spiritual universe, sin is not seen in the same way as it is here. In the spirit world, all things are learning experiences. We are here in this world to make mistakes, to learn and grow from them.

-- Near-Death Experiencer Jayne Smith

210

I was shown how every single individual through their own free will chooses paths that MATHEMATICALLY take them to the circumstances of their next existence or life; that NOTHING at all sits in accident or chaos; that every single aspect of our lives is ruled by NATURAL laws that we placed ourselves in; that in a sense, we create our own worlds.

-- Near-Death Experiencer Amy Call

211

I cannot describe the relief, the refreshing, peaceful balm this knowledge was for me; to finally gather this truth that I'd yearned for all of my life: that all is good; that there is sense and beauty all around; that no one is just "free-falling" as it had seemed before; that God doesn't just get to toy with us as He pleases with random ideas of tests, including rewards and punishments that just depend upon His current mood or mindset. While in this experience, out in the vast expanse of stars and planets, moons, and knowledge, I knew complete trust for what felt like the first time. This was bliss for me. I had lived in fear, distrust, and panic for 30 years.

-- Near-Death Experiencer Amy Call

212

As outrageous as it may seem to our perspective in the physical, the man who built the bomb that blew me up may have performed that action at my own request. This is not to imply that because it was at my request, his actions are acceptable within the physical world and ought to be overlooked. The role may have been agreed upon in order for the bomber himself to experience what it's like to be chased, arrested, detained, or killed for the violence he visited on others. The bomber's actions don't have to be condoned in the physical world, because he and I as Whole Selves agreed to blow me up; we all keep playing our roles within the context of the physical (the collective reality that we as Whole Selves have chosen to focus upon and participate in) according to what we think is good and right.

That as a Whole Being, I actually chose to be blown up, flies in the face of more than one cultural base assumption. We generally assume that things happen to us and that there are many things that we simply can't control. Accidents happen, mistakes are made, some people are lucky, and some are not. My experience simply doesn't support this base assumption. Whether consciously aware of it in the physical mind or not, my

Whole Self is fully aware of every experience as a cooperative effort between my focused awareness within the physical world, my Whole Self, and other individual Selves. I craft my physical experiences. Things don't happen to me without my consent; they happen because I created, co-created, or agreed to experience them.

-- Near-Death Experiencer Natalie Sudman

213

My Guide lovingly stayed as my support while I had a kind of Life Review... I was being given the opportunity and the gift of being able to stand back and more fully understand and love myself... I understood how everything I did and said, and even thought, had touched others around me in one way or another. More than anything, I could feel how child-like everyone was. With every person I viewed, including myself, I was able to see and feel with a Higher Mind and Eye. And the feeling I had toward everyone was nothing less than what a loving mother would feel for her children at toddler age.

-- Near-Death Experiencer Amy Call

214

It was actually comical at times. I could feel how the "Elders," as I will call them, see us and find so much humor in the way we do things. The Elders view these things very much like when a mother sees her two-year-old scream and cry and bop another child on the head with a stuffed animal. The mother doesn't want her child to "fall apart" and become hysterical and cry. She feels for her child, but at the same time, she sees a little bit of comedy in how seriously the child takes what is usually a trivial drama. She continues to love her child and thinks the world of it, hoping it will go on enjoying the day, living and learning.

-- Near-Death Experiencer Amy Call

215

I was able to explore the mind or energetic pattern of one of my life's sworn enemies -- someone I couldn't imagine forgiving for what I'd witnessed. And yet, coming back from my NDE, I could feel nothing more than a flood of Love for this woman that I dived in at the chance to write her a letter and tell her how much I loved her, and to ask for forgiveness for the energetic weight I might have held over her from my own dark thoughts and anger. She could have been my own firstborn. That is how much I adored her at that time. Because I was able to feel the Divine Love for her that God feels toward her, I too, couldn't help but love her in a similar way. It was such a surprisingly marvelous feeling to relinquish the burden of my own anger and judgments.

-- Near-Death Experiencer Amy Call

216

I felt a Higher part of me that had compassion for the me that was so ignorant and juvenile. It seemed to understand what I was working with, in every detail, and it only wanted for my joy.

-- Near-Death Experiencer Amy Call

217

I trusted and knew that everything was in its right place . . . even when people made decisions that I didn't agree with, I still felt that in the overall picture, it was ALL "Good."

-- Near-Death Experiencer Amy Call

218

I lost all desire to judge every little thing as being either "good" or "bad." I wasn't concerned. We are all just consciousness experiencing life, and learning how to love, create, and develop to the Highest we can be. I knew to choose what felt right for me and to trust more; that when something felt unjust or imbalanced, to do what I could to work toward harmony, but to not worry about that which I had no control over. I know that eventually, even without our taking over the controls, the Universe is so full of Order, it always finds a way to Balance everything, because the Universe cannot exist without perfect Balance. And it will continue to exist.

-- Near-Death Experiencer Amy Call

219

Learn to get in touch with silence within yourself and know that everything in life has a purpose.

-- Near-Death Experience Researcher Elisabeth Kubler-Ross

220

We're so used to thinking in terms of hierarchies. The healer is more important than the addict. The teacher is more important than the arms dealer. These hierarchies of values are not real. I don't care how dull, or weird, or messed up we think our lives are here in the physical world, I can assure you that all of us are having a valuable experience. And I don't care how special we think we are; we are each uniquely special. Every single one of us. Our experience extends and enhances everything that exists. We are each infinitely creative beings having an amazing experience just by being here.

-- Near-Death Experiencer Natalie Sudman

221

Imagine that everything you have ever thought, imagined, experienced, dreamed, or created was recognized to be valuable to yourself and to everyone else -- to all that exists. Imagine that no matter what you do or how you express yourself, you belong and are valued. This is true. What was known to me, what was so basic as to be assumed was just that: we are each intrinsically valuable and everything we experience matters, not just to ourselves but to each other and to All That Is.

-- Near-Death Experiencer Natalie Sudman

222

I saw purpose in every event of my entire life. I saw how every circumstance had been divinely provided for my learning and development. I had the realization that I had actually taken part in creating every experience of my life. I knew I had come to this Earth for only one reason, which was to learn, and that everything that had ever happened to me had been a loving step in that process of my progression. Every person, every circumstance, and every incident, was custom created for me. It was as if the entire universe existed for my higher good and development. I felt so loved, so cherished, and so honored.

-- Near-Death Experiencer Jeff Olsen

223

I knew that there are no accidents in this life; that everything happens for a reason . . . Everything suddenly made sense. Everything had Divine order.

-- Near-Death Experiencer Jeff Olsen

224

There are no mistakes, no coincidences. All events are blessings given to us to learn.

-- Near-Death Experience Researcher Elisabeth Kubler-Ross

225

I saw that truly nothing happens by accident or luck, but everything by God's wise providence. If it seems to be accident or luck from our point of view, our blindness and lack of foreknowledge is the cause; for matters that have been in God's foreseeing wisdom since before time began befall us suddenly, all unawares; and so in our blindness and ignorance we say that this is accident or luck, but to our Lord God it is not so.

-- Near-Death Experiencer Julian of Norwich

226

Our reasoning powers are so blind now, so humble, and so simple, that we cannot know the high, marvelous wisdom; the might and the goodness of God.

-- Near-Death Experiencer Julian of Norwich

227

All shall be well, and all shall be well, and all manner of thing shall be well.

-- Near-Death Experiencer Julian of Norwich

228

Everything is in perfect order no matter what it looks like here.

-- Near-Death Experiencer Jeff Olsen

229

Everything was so miraculous. Every moment. Every breath that's happening. Every connection we make personally is just the most beautiful, miraculous thing. If we could see what was really going on behind all of this and how much is involved in each one of us and how beautiful it really is -- the bigger picture -- we would really just be in awe all the time. I can see why maybe we need not to be in this state all the time, because I couldn't even function. I was going from laughing to crying and things like that. People could have legitimately said "She needs to be locked up," and I would probably have understood.

-- Near-Death Experiencer Amy Call

230

We (here on Earth) have a role to play. We choose our lives even before we are born -- whether we chose a good life or a bad one, it matters not, because there is NO good or bad. It's just your chosen role. ALL lives lived are essential for our evolution and development . . . Sorry to say this, BUT even the most evil -- death, destruction, disease -- is essential! Think about it: if everything was ALWAYS good and going your way; if all relationships were good and everyone got what they wanted, over the years it would get pretty boring and stagnant. I know it sounds wonderful, but it wouldn't let us grow much, would it?

-- IANDS Near-Death Experiencer #3

231

During the review of my life, Jesus repeatedly allowed me to see both the immediate and distant effects of an event. I was able to appreciate and understand how each event spread through time and space, initiating a cascade of other events from which something of beauty and worth always emerged.

-- Near-Death Experiencer Mary Neal, MD

232

One of God's most astonishing gifts is His ability to use time to heal and redeem: to make something beautiful later out of something that appears ugly now.

-- Near-Death Experiencer Mary Neal, MD

233

Does God really work all things together for our good? During my Life Review, as I witnessed beauty emerging from every event, my faith in God's promise shifted from a somewhat vague theological hope into complete trust. I understood that He genuinely does make everything beautiful in His time.

-- Near-Death Experiencer Mary Neal, MD

234

I began to believe that nature had made a mistake and that human beings were probably a cancerous organism on the planet. I saw no way that we could get out from all the problems we had created for ourselves and the planet. I perceived all humans as cancer, and that is what I got. That is what killed me. Be careful what your world view is. It can feed back on you, especially if it is a negative world view. I had a seriously negative one. That is what led me into my death.

-- Near-Death Experiencer Mellen-Thomas Benedict

235

I asked God, "Why would You create humanity? Why would humanity be created when they are such dark and evil beings?"

The Light turned into a mandala, like a big, round stained-glass window that was alive, and I was breathed into the center of it. In that center, it was like I could look into every human soul, including my own. I could see no evil at all. No darkness in any human that has ever lived. That may shock you. It shocked me. But I was there in the nexus, the mandala of human souls. There was something in us all -- and in all of nature and all of Gaia -- that's incorruptible, no matter what you've ever done -- it's incorruptible. That is that Source in you that is perfect, that is there already. In that moment, I heard The Light say, "Oh Beautiful Human." It was a blessing. And in that moment, I fell in love with humanity again. I think that's when my cancer was cured.

-- Near-Death Experiencer Mellen-Thomas Benedict

236

Look, if you study near-death experiences carefully, all kinds of human assumptions are challenged. We're told time doesn't actually exist. That the world is an illusion. That the universe, both what we can see with our physical eyes and what lies beyond our five senses, is full of life, some of which is unimaginably weird. We're told that we are all accountable for everything we do. That all life is connected. That God loves everyone, wholeheartedly and unconditionally, including rapists, murderers, and people like Adolph Hitler, Joseph Stalin, and Mao Tse Tung. There are hellish realms and demonic beings. There are heavenly realms for all kinds of believers, not just Christians. There are also Christians, who thought they were living good, Christian lives, in hell. And on and on and on. There is pretty much something to offend everyone. I'm not making the rules. I'm not trying to justify what NDEs tell us. I'm trying to understand. And even that's a problem, because NDEs also tell us, point blank, that the system is designed to be beyond human comprehension. We're not supposed to be able to remember who we are, where we are really from, and how everything works. That's a foundational rule of the game. Near-death experiencers regularly report becoming omniscient and while in that exalted state, knowing how everything works. And it's beautiful. It's Perfect. It's breathtakingly wonderful. And then that awareness is snatched away, and they are stuffed back into fragile bodies and tiny brains that can't figure out how to deal with doctors who want to commit them to mental institutions, husbands and wives who abandon them, and careers that fall apart.

I'm sorry. There are no easy answers. If we want to understand what NDEs are about, we have to learn how to swim in waters that are deeply disturbing to ordinary human sensibilities. And that takes time, patience, and effort. And a whole new set of skills that are completely alien to normal, everyday life.

-- Near-Death Experience Researcher David Sunfellow

THE WISDOM & POWER OF NDES

-Seven-
Delusions Of Grandeur

People who have dramatic spiritual experiences often believe themselves to be more evolved, more perfect, more godlike than they actually are. This delusion needs to be nipped in the bud before immature egos turn into giant hot air balloons...

237

After my near-death experience, I wrongly assumed that I was going to be a saint. That I would not have a temper, anger, or lust, or make mistakes at all. That somehow, I had been elevated to this superior person. To my horror, I found out that wasn't the case at all.

-- Near-Death Experiencer Howard Storm

238

[After my near-death experience], I was a raging fanatic. I drove my wife and my two teenage children very far away from me by being so obnoxious about their conversion.

-- Near-Death Experiencer Howard Storm

239

I've been on this journey for 40 years. I had my NDE in 1975. I see the NDE as the beginning, and this journey is an adventure that never ends. Enlightenment is a fantasy -- as soon as someone announces they are enlightened, they "fall" because the label energizes the ego.

-- Near-Death Experiencer Barbara Harris Whitfield

240

I've seen it over and over. Experiencers become arrogant -- they've got the answers, and everyone should listen to them, which is the worst way to handle our relationships. We used to call it the "Guru Syndrome." Humility means having the willingness and openness to learn more about self, others, and the God of our Understanding.

-- Near-Death Experiencer Barbara Harris Whitfield

241

A large number of near-death experiencers report that they felt one of the reasons they had their experience was because they had lost their way in life. Because of this, they required a major wake-up call, which is what their near-death experience gave them. A wake-up call does not turn formerly dysfunctional people into healthy people. It gives them a story to share, a map to follow, and concrete ways to begin to tackle all the areas of their lives and personalities that require deepening and healing. What this means is that near-death experiencers, while they often have wonderful stories to tell, including stories of miraculous healings and newfound paranormal abilities, are not necessarily the wisest, healthiest, most evolved people.

-- Near-Death Experience Researcher David Sunfellow

242

Here is a universal truth that everyone needs to know: Spiritual experiences, including near-death experiences, DO NOT perfect the human side of our nature. Spiritual experiences can, however, blind us and make us (and others) think we are more developed than we actually are. If we focus too much on the spiritual realities of life without focusing enough on the imperfect, growing, evolving human side of ourselves; if we discount, ignore, or suppress the shadowy, undeveloped sides of our nature, these forces will eventually catch up with us and set our earthly lives on fire.

-- Near-Death Experience Researcher David Sunfellow

243

To those who are looking to near-death experiencers as emissaries of The Divine: Yes, near-death experiencers have been sent back, in part, to share their stories and, by doing so, help illuminate all of us. Beyond that, near-death experiencers may or may not be able to offer solid, seasoned advice. Along with integrating whatever spiritual experiences they had into daily life, it often takes decades of daily work on shadow and developmental issues to create vessels that allow The Divine to emerge in us in healthy, balanced, full blown ways. The same is true for us. Like near-death experiencers, we must also work on ourselves, which includes not giving our power and personal responsibility away to others who appear to be more evolved than we are.

-- Near-Death Experience Researcher David Sunfellow

244

As always, discrimination and discernment must be exercised, because even in "the near-death world" . . . there are persons, including some NDErs, who are not always what they seem, or who suffer from obvious self-inflation or other grandiose tendencies that any prudent person would do well to eschew immediately . . . Please remember something that should be obvious: NDErs, though they may have seen The Light, are still human and have human failings. Not they, but only The Light should be exalted. So do not let your enthusiasm for these teachings and for what The Light represents blind you to possible excesses in Its name.

-- Near-Death Experience Researcher Kenneth Ring, PhD

245

Not everyone who claims they had a near-death experience actually had one. And those who have had near-death experiences sometimes embellish their accounts.

-- Near-Death Experience Researcher David Sunfellow

246

To weed out fabrications and embellishments, it is helpful to study near-death experiences as a whole rather than rely on singular accounts from specific individuals, time periods, and cultures.

-- Near-Death Experience Researcher David Sunfellow

247

No single experiencer can supply all the answers! The power of the near-death phenomenon and what it can tell us can best be found through a synthesis or summary of the many. True, just being around an experiencer, or reading experiencer books, can be life changing. I grant you that. But transferring to any experiencer the role of speaking for everyone else, or being the best speaker, or having the most to say, or holding the record for the most harrowing case, or being the most angelic, or gifted, or blessed, or verified, or stunning, is tantamount to self-deception.

-- Near-Death Experiencer and Researcher P.M.H. Atwater

248

We are masters of self-deception. If there is anything that human beings are good at, it's self-deception.

-- Near-Death Experiencer Howard Storm

249

Here are two reasons it is important for anyone who has had a near-death experience, or spiritually transformative experience, to learn about the experiences of others: Along with making it crystal clear that we aren't the messiahs we might think we are (because the bus is full of other people who have had experiences as deep, or deeper than our own), learning about the experiences of others gives us a small taste of just how big the universe is and how teeny weeny our current understandings are.

-- Near-Death Experience Researcher David Sunfellow

250

Some of today's new crop of near-death experiencers are far too willing to come across as blanket authorities on the subject, and they are equally much too anxious to present "one-sized-fits-all" answers to life's greatest questions.

-- Near-Death Experiencer and Researcher P.M.H Atwater

251

Humility is one of the best, most accurate measurements of spiritual maturity.

The reverse is also true.

-- Near-Death Experience Researcher David Sunfellow

252

Humility isn't the cure for experiencers becoming arrogant, IMO. Honesty is. Humility will come when one is completely honest with their self. But it's a rare individual that is honest, at least with their self. Most can't stand to look in the mirror that intently.

-- Near-Death Experiencer Don O'Conner

253

The way I see it, a spiritual experience is meaningless unless it's applied. Constricted unless it's shared. Perverted if it's used for self-aggrandization or personal material benefit. Perhaps only if we rise above these normal human failings do we breathe life into our near-death experiences.

-- Near-Death Experiencer Rajiv Sinha, MD

254

I tend to trust early near-death experience accounts more than recent ones for two reasons: 1. Early experiencers were not influenced by the accounts of others (because other accounts were unknown); 2. People who shared their experiences before NDEs were widely known and accepted, were often attacked, ridiculed, and marginalized. That's still happening today, of course, but the dangers were more acute in the early years. There were also less rewards and incentives. Today, you can become a best-selling author, a famous personality, a spiritual teacher and leader, overnight, and not have every aspect of your personal life and story scrutinized. In years past, you were more likely to be institutionalized, lose your job and family, and be cast to the outer edges of society. Sharing your story in the early years, in other words, was a real act of bravery. And most people don't willingly step into firestorms, unless they feel compelled by deeper forces to do so.

-- Near-Death Experience Researcher David Sunfellow

255

Generally speaking, we should be more focused on becoming embodiments of love than speaking and writing about it.

-- Near-Death Experience Researcher David Sunfellow

256

The message that these children were telling me [children who had near-death experiences] is that we're here for a reason. This reality is a school and we're here to learn lessons of love. I lectured on this. I told people this . . . I felt that I was just so filled with wisdom and helping grieving parents and all of this. And yet, in my personal life, things were really deteriorating, and I did not learn my lessons of love. To make a long story short, I did this myself, I created a very toxic, ugly environment in my personal life, and this resulted in my stepdaughter making false accusations against me. These accusations resulted in my being convicted of child endangerment. It was very dramatic. Headlines all over the country. Pediatrician waterboards his stepdaughter. At first, I couldn't believe that people really took that seriously, because oddly enough, I was never accused of waterboarding her. But I was convicted, and I spent two years in prison.

-- Near-Death Experience Researcher Melvin Morse, MD

257

Everyone carries a shadow, and the less it is embodied in the individual's conscious life, the blacker and denser it is.

-- Near-Death Experiencer Carl Jung

258

Those who don't work on shadow issues either become a wolf in sheep's clothing or get eaten by one.

-- Near-Death Experience Researcher David Sunfellow

259

I want to be a common man. I don't want to pretend to be a saint. My aspiration is to be authentic, and I find that to be a real struggle. One of the things that I think is a huge problem with near-death experiencers, and I include myself in that category . . . is egotism. I've been turned off by some near-death experiencers because their ego was getting in the way of their truth and their authenticity.

-- Near-Death Experiencer Howard Storm

260

Learn from those who have gone before you -- study their lives, visions, discoveries, challenges, successes, and failures. Consider their advice carefully. Follow your own path, but don't walk it alone. Isolation leads to stagnation, blindness, and an inflated sense of self-importance. Don't think you have all the answers (even if your experience may have led you to believe you do). Assume others see and understand things you don't. Also assume that you have blind spots and weaknesses that others can see more clearly than you can. Pay attention when others trigger your fears, shortcomings, and inadequacies. If you get upset, angry, or defensive, good. Welcome inner storms. Follow them back to their source. When you discover the true source of unsettled feelings, new heights, depths, and vistas will open up to you. Be brave. Be bold. Be humble. Surround yourself with truth tellers; avoid zombies, groupies, and yes people. And, as much as possible, tell the truth, first to yourself and then to as many others as you can without being inappropriate or causing unnecessary harm. If your heart is in the right place, your mind will follow and everything in your life will get better, cleaner, healthier.

-- Near-Death Experience Researcher David Sunfellow

-Eight-
Paradise Lost

Visiting Heaven is easy. Staying in Heaven -- or, more accurately, bringing Heaven to Earth, in human bodies and minds -- requires epic levels of personal development...

261

I felt like I was not even human anymore, that I had been changed somehow into this spiritual being that walks through life and would look up at the sky and see the trees and feel this amazing, amazing love that God has. It was permeating EVERYTHING. It was in the rocks. It was in the trees and I could feel it. I walked around in this bliss cloud for two weeks just knowing God and feeling His love so profoundly. And then it started to fade, and I freaked out and I started to pray: "Heavenly Father, why, why are you pulling away? Am I not being good enough? Is something wrong?"

And He said, "Ryan, I've carried you for two weeks. Now I am walking beside you. You need to learn and reach out and learn how to bring me into you. And how to encourage the relationship we have with each other."

And so that was the next part of my journey...

THE WISDOM & POWER OF NDES

-- Near-Death Experiencer Ryan Rampton

262

I felt like trillions of billions of gigabytes of information were being downloaded to me . . . I was able to see God's wisdom and derive pleasure . . . I didn't have the ability to sustain it. It just washed me. I didn't have the vessel to actually hold that information. As it was going, as pleasurable as it was, there was also a tremendous feeling of the opposite of pleasure, that I can't hold it, that I can't sustain it, that I can't grasp it and keep it. It says in many sources that our acts in this world create a spiritual vessel that when our soul leaves the body it has the tool to actually hold that Godly life, to hold that Godly revelation, to be able to hold that Godly wisdom. I wasn't able to hold it. I was able to see it. I was able to enjoy it. But I wasn't able to hold it. So simultaneously it was a tremendous feeling of pleasure, and at the same time, this very strong feeling of the opposite of pleasure . . . Almost like taking a little kid to a toy store and letting him run there and at the end of it, telling him, "OK, now we have to go home and you can't keep any of the toys. You have to leave all the toys here. Now it's time to go home."

-- Near-Death Experiencer Alon Anava

263

One of the issues I've had for years and years since is that I get really frustrated that I can't feel God on command in every situation anymore. I don't live in bliss all the time like I did after my NDE. This "failing" of mine has caused me a lot of distress. I couldn't make sense of why I would be given such a vision, such an experience, such a profound awakening, only to lose it, or have it yanked away, leaving me only with a memory of what I used to know and live and feel.

-- Near-Death Experiencer Amphianda Baskett

264

As my physical state became one of recovery rather than survival, I was more fully absorbed back into the reality of this world. My ties with God's world became less palpable, until I was no longer able to pass between worlds or have conversations with angels.

-- Near-Death Experiencer Mary Neal, MD

265

What happened following that miraculous experience? Well, just as my life preview showed me, I lost all my friends because they thought I was crazy. My family didn't believe me either. Some people mocked me as I told them about my experience. A Baptist minister told me never to speak of this experience again because Satan was working through me.

-- Near-Death Experiencer Nancy Clark

266

"The moment I woke up from the coma, I knew that I'd believed a lie . . . People would fill the churches to hear this [lie]. I had a very charismatic personality. It seemed the less I preached love, the busier I stayed . . . I can't tell those lies anymore. I can't preach that crap. I hurt thousands of people."

-- Near-Death Experience Researcher John W. Price quoting a hellfire and damnation preacher who had a near-death experience that taught him that God was loving and forgiving. The preacher lost his ministry when his congregation refused to abandon their belief in a wrathful, vindictive God who hates sinners.

267

[After my NDE] I was so young, and innocent, and full of love -- this 22-year-old young woman -- and I was oblivious to the darkness; I was oblivious to how to protect myself in this world. I think part of my work is to remind young near-death experiencers how to protect themselves. Part of my story is a tough story. I lived in this blissful, happy state of connection with everyone. I loved teaching and I loved my life so much, but when I was in South Korea, I was asleep in my bed and an acquaintance of a friend came in and raped me. I was shocked and horrified... I didn't know why I was fated to have that [experience] until years later many of my students -- male and female, even young boys and young girls -- would come to me and tell me their stories of being molested or raped . . . They were drawn to me. I was a safe person that they could talk to. So [everything came] full circle ... I realized whatever our wounds are, they prepare us to be stronger and more loving in this world. What I didn't receive, I can now give to others.

-- Near-Death Experiencer Tricia Barker

268

If you're pining to have a near-death experience ... I would say don't! This is not what you want. It may seem like a blessing, but it is often [as much] a curse, as it is a blessing. It leaves one disassociated. It leaves one depressed. I went through a long period of depression. I live a life of non-attachment, not detachment, but non-attachment. My connectivity is to the other side, not so much here.

-- Near-Death Experiencer Peter Panagore

269

When snatched from the jaws of death, tooth marks are to be expected.

-- Near-Death Experiencer Hal Story

270

Most people, when they hear or read accounts of NDEs, feel a certain amount of envy, wishing that they too could have the experience (without, to be sure, having to go to the trouble of nearly dying for the privilege). But if they could really get under the skin and into the psyche of the NDEr, they would soon realize that the NDE is often a mixed blessing and may continue to extract a high cost in suffering from the individual's life.

-- Near-Death Experience Researcher Kenneth Ring, PhD

271

I can't tell you how many times I hear "I want the NDE without the ND [near death] part." But there's lots of ways to remember who we are. You don't need to do the ND part. A lot of people want the flashy, spiritually transformative experience of an NDE or something that happens that changes their whole life in an instant. Well, when you have that, unless you have already done the work before you had that experience, you're going to have to do that work after that experience.

-- Near-Death Experiencer Natalie Sudman

272

A spiritually transformative experience is not always just magic. It can be very disruptive. And very, very difficult afterwards. It may not always be, but it can be. "Be careful what you wish for," is what I am saying. [A flashy, spiritual experience] may not be the best way for you. You may be working your way along slowly, slowly, and you may be a lot farther along than you think you are. Just keep going. It's your path. It's your path, and your path is valuable for you. Their path is not valuable for you.

-- Near-Death Experiencer Natalie Sudman

273

Most NDErs have a difficult time coming to terms with their experience, and the process of its integration into their lives may take a long time -- and, certainly, in some cases, it does not occur at all. Longstanding relationships may be strained to and beyond the breaking point, marriages collapse, misunderstandings are common, and periods of painful introspection and even depression are not rare. The NDE, as we have seen, tends to turn a person's life topsy-turvy, and the radical reorientation and personal courage to live out the truth of one's NDE may be very taxing indeed, both to the NDEr and his or her family and friends.

-- Near-Death Experience Researcher Kenneth Ring, PhD

274

I hear from people all the time who want to have near-death experiences. They want to experience an NDE so they can experience the positive aftereffects that are associated with these experiences. They forget, or may not know, that many negative or challenging aftereffects are also associated with NDEs, not the least of which is learning how to integrate the newfound energies and visions into their day-to-day lives and personalities.

-- Near-Death Experience Researcher David Sunfellow

275

The greater the distance between our earthly personality and the heights we reach during a spiritual experience, the greater the reckoning when we return. Because of this, my advice is simple: don't waste your time longing for near-death experiences (or any other kind of spiritually transformative experience). Instead, do the daily, challenging, unglamorous work of becoming a better, kinder, healthier, more loving and compassionate person -- step by step, little by little. And let the spiritual experiences take care of themselves.

-- Near-Death Experience Researcher David Sunfellow

276

Unless we've built a consciousness that can handle, channel, and ground high voltage spiritual experiences, these experiences will blow fuses all over the place, and there will be a lot of cleanup work once the smoke clears.

-- Near-Death Experience Researcher David Sunfellow

277

To the extent you . . . try to live in accordance with the lessons and values of the NDE, you can expect to confront difficulties and unexpected challenges. Do not think, for instance, that your family and friends will necessarily approve of or even understand your new behavior and attitudes. Do not suppose for a moment that you will not experience inner conflict, and even a significant degree of emotional turmoil, as these changes begin to take root in you. Change is hard and change without a significant degree of social support is even harder. If you want the benefits of the NDE, however, you will have to work for them and overcome the resistance you will encounter. Our society, after all, while it may accord nominal approval to many of the ideals of the NDE, often undermines them in practice. Even a moment's reflection on the behavioral implications of the NDE is sufficient to convince most people that the NDE is itself a subversive phenomenon in the sense that it undercuts the crasser forms of the American Dream. Swim in the current of the NDE for long and you will find yourself encountering powerful opposing forces. Be prepared for them and seek shelter when necessary.

-- Near-Death Experience Researcher Kenneth Ring, PhD

− Nine −
Suicide

Whether we are a near-death experiencer who longs to return to The Light, or a human being that has been beaten down by the challenges of life, suicide, with few exceptions, is not the way to solve our problems. Suicide can actually make our difficulties much worse...

278

In my research base of 277 child experiencers, 21 percent attempted suicide within about eight years to get back to The Other Side. None of those I had sessions with thought they were doing anything negative or hurtful by taking such action; they just wanted to return to the bright worlds -- the place of their homey Home.

-- Near-Death Experience Researcher P.M.H. Atwater

279

It took my spirit longer to recover than my body, though that in itself was a long time. I was very depressed, for many years, and often dealt with suicidal thoughts because the desire to be "Home" was so great. I was confused for the longest time. I was afraid. I found being in a body painful, restricting, and limiting. I am still greatly uncomfortable with it.

-- IANDS Near-Death Experiencer #6

280

It is important to be here ... There's a purpose for coming back. For me, it's being a source of that Divine love. It's showing people what it was like to be in Heaven, what it can be for us to be a positive source of love ... Every night for months I prayed that I would die. Every night . . . until I realized the main purpose for me was sharing love.

-- Near-Death Experiencer Nancy Rynes

281

Have you ever interviewed anyone who has had a near-death experience in association with a suicide attempt? If so, was the experience any different?

I do know of a few cases in which a suicide attempt was the cause of the apparent "death." These experiences were uniformly characterized as being unpleasant.

As one woman said, "If you leave here a tormented soul, you will be a tormented soul over there, too." In short, they report that the conflicts they had attempted suicide to escape were still present when they died, but with added complications. In their disembodied state they were unable to do anything about their problems, and they also had to view the unfortunate consequences which resulted from their acts.

-- Near-Death Experience Researcher Raymond Moody, MD

282

Dr. Kenneth Ring, in his book, *Life at Death*, analyzed the near-death experiences of 24 people who attempted suicide. Among them, no one reported the tunnel phenomenon, or saw a brilliant but comforting light, or encountered a presence, or was temporarily reunited with loved ones who had died, or entered into a transcendent world of heavenly beauty. Instead, the suicide-related NDE tended to be truncated, aborted, and damped down. It began with a feeling of relief or peace and continued with a sense of bodily detachment to the same degree as non-suicide-related NDEs. But it tended to end, if it got this far at all, with a feeling of confused drifting in a dark or murky void -- a sort of twilight zone. Dr. Ring's research strongly suggests that the suicide-related NDE does not reach completion; instead, it tends simply to fade out before the transcendent elements characteristic of non-suicide related NDEs make their appearance...

In Dr. Kenneth Ring's study, he found that no one who had attempted suicide reported that it was predominately unpleasant. The only possible exception is that a few people did describe some unsettling hallucinatory images, but these appear to have been qualitatively different from the feeling-tone of non-suicidal experiences. Certainly, no one felt that he was either in or was on his way to hell. This is not to say that suicide attempts never lead to unpleasant experiences, only that there is no strong evidence for this proposition among the 24 suicide NDEs in Dr. Ring's study.

-- Near-Death Experience Researcher Kevin Williams

283

I have found one positive side to my suicide attempt. Now, when people come to me with suicidal thoughts, I can talk to them with firsthand knowledge about this horrible urge. I freely share my own story of attempted suicide and tell them why I am glad I didn't succeed. I also bring in the data about people who have tried to commit suicide and had near-death experiences before being revived. These people say that they will never again try to kill themselves, not because they fear going to hell, but because they have learned that life does have a purpose.

-- Near-Death Experience Researcher Raymond Moody, MD

284

Scientific studies of spiritually transformative experiences, particularly research focused on near-death experiences occurring to persons who have survived suicide attempts, tell us that those who commit suicide deeply regret the choice they made to end their own life. They wish they could take it back and find a way to persevere against all obstacles, no matter how great.

-- Near-Death Experiencer and Researcher Eben Alexander, MD

285

Dr. Raymond Moody has reported that one of the few categorically true observations to be made about suicide is that, if one attempts suicide and experiences any of the features of an NDE (encountering brilliant light and an overwhelming sense of a divine force of love in the universe, meeting souls of departed loved ones, etc.), then he or she will never attempt suicide again.

-- Near-Death Experiencer and Researcher Eben Alexander, MD

286

Due to the overwhelming percentage of loving and warm experiences reported in near-death experiences, I occasionally receive emails from people, often in a depression, wondering if they should try suicide in order to induce one. I immediately respond: "Absolutely not!" I encourage those who are depressed to seek counseling and also to discuss their life issues with their health-care team. People who had near-death experiences as a result of suicide attempts almost uniformly later believe that their suicide attempts were serious mistakes. An NDE should never be sought by creating a life-threatening event.

-- Near-Death Experience Researcher Jeffrey Long, MD

287

NDE reports ... suggest that during the Life Review, those who succeed at suicide likely witness a profound sense of love that others and the universe at large have for them, and gain comfort from that revelation, but they also realize the deep pain that many felt in their loss.

-- Near-Death Experiencer and Researcher Eben Alexander, MD

288

Near-death experiences reveal the quality of our lives after death is not determined by how we die, but by how we live. Unfortunately, many suicides cause devastating emotional damage to families lasting a lifetime or more. This is the REAL tragedy and the problem with committing suicide. While near-death experiences show that suicide, in itself, has spiritual consequences, which are no different from other ways of dying, it does show there are penalties for hurting others. This is why people who decide to justifiably end their life must do the research and prepare themselves and those around them.

-- Near-Death Experience Researcher Kevin Williams

289

Near-Death Experiencer Angie Fenimore ended up in a hellish realm after a suicide attempt. She wrote a book about her experience for two reasons: To help people understand that "suicide is not a solution" and that heavenly realms are not the only places people go when they die. People can also end up in hellish realms like she did.

1. "Suicide is not a solution. I don't care what your belief system is. Whatever it is, suicide is just not a solution, because that's just not how -- look for the evidence around you -- that's not how it works."

2. "It was seeing all these so-called positive near-death experiences where people go to a pillar of light, tunnel of light, all that, and I knew that's not the only way that it can go. I felt completely, strongly that people need to know that it's not always like that."

-- Near-Death Experiencer Angie Fenimore

290

As my Life Review continued, I encountered again all of the pain and hopelessness of my next several years; a series of bad relationships, pregnancies, miscarriages, broken marriages and suicide attempts. I saw myself as a young woman of twenty-five, married and divorced three times and hospitalized for drug overdoses six times. I felt how I hated my existence and could not understand how a loving God could allow these things to happen.

I was aware as I relived each of these terribly painful events in my life that the Light, which was with me as I watched, felt all of my pain and sorrow and never judged me, but instead understood and loved me.

The love I felt from The Light was overwhelming, and I never wanted to leave It. While I was in Its presence, I had unlimited knowledge about anything I wanted to know. I was given the choice of remaining with The Light, provided I return later to the physical world and experience all that brought me to the point of shooting myself, or I could return now and pick up my life where it was. I was told that I would eventually have the family and love I so desperately yearned for. I was also told that I could only take back the knowledge I needed to sustain myself, although I would be given insights to help others and me along the way as I continued my life journey.

-- Near-Death Experiencer Sandra Rogers

291

Suicide is like dropping out of a college course in the middle of the semester. If you want credit for the course, you must take it again from the beginning, and keep going until completion.

-- Near-Death Experiencer Sandra Rogers

292

Dr. George Ritchie, author of *Return From Tomorrow* and *My Life After Dying*, learned during his near-death experience what happens to some people who commit suicide. According to Ritchie, the quality of life a person initially finds after suicide is influenced by their motive for committing it. He classifies suicide in the following three ways:

1. The first classification are those people who kill themselves in order to hurt someone, get revenge, or who kill themselves out of anger for someone else. They arrive in the earthbound realm out of hatred, jealousy, resentment, bitterness and total distain for themselves and others. Ritchie writes, "I want to make clear that it was impressed upon me that these were the ones who had the same type of powerful emotions which people who committed murder have." Ritchie says such people mistakenly believe they are not committing murder which their religious training tells them is a worse sin than suicide. Their motive for killing themselves is, "If I can't kill you, I will kill myself to get even with you." According to Ritchie, such people "haunt" the living by being aware of every horrible consequence their suicide had on others.

2. The second classification includes those who, because of mental illness, confusion, or a terminal illness, take their own life. Ritchie states these people are allowed many opportunities from God to grow in love just as any other person would who

had not committed suicide. In other words, there are no negative consequences for them.

3. The third classification includes those who kill themselves from drug, alcohol, or any other addiction. According to Ritchie, these people can become stuck in limbo trying in vain to satisfy their addiction until eventually something frees them. This condition is also called an earthbound condition.

Concerning souls belonging to the first classification, Ritchie writes:

"I understood from what I was seeing that these people and the average murderer also are confined in a state where they are given a chance to realize two very important facts: One, you can only kill the body, not the soul. Two, that only love, not hate, can bring them and others true happiness. I believe once they fully understand this, they are given the opportunity to continue their spiritual and mental growth."

-- Near-Death Experience Researcher Kevin Williams

293

My most dramatic and unforgettable case of "ask and you will be given," and also of a near-death experience, was a man who was in the process of being picked up by his entire family for a Memorial Day weekend drive to visit some relatives out of town. While driving in the family van to pick him up, his parents-in-law with his wife and eight children were hit by a gasoline tanker. The gasoline poured over the car and burned his entire family to death. After being told what happened, this man remained in a state of total shock and numbness for several weeks. He stopped working and was unable to communicate. To make a long story short, he became a total bum, drinking half-a-gallon of whisky a day, trying heroin and other drugs to numb his pain. He was unable to hold a job for any length of time and ended up literally in the gutter.

It was during one of my hectic traveling tours, having just finished the second lecture in a day on life after death, that a hospice group in Santa Barbara asked me to give yet another lecture. After my preliminary statements, I became aware that I am very tired of repeating the same stories over and over again. And I quietly said to myself:

"Oh God, why don't you send me somebody from the audience who has had a near-death experience and is willing to share it with the audience so I can take a break? They will have a first-hand experience instead of hearing my old stories over and over again."

At that very moment the organizer of the group gave me a little slip of paper with an urgent message on it. It was a message from a man from the bowery who begged to share his near-death experience with me. I took a little break and sent a messenger to his bowery hotel. A few moments later, after a speedy cab ride, the man appeared in the audience. Instead of being a bum as he had described himself, he was a rather well dressed, very sophisticated man. He went up on the stage and without having a need to evaluate him, I encouraged him to tell the audience what he needed to share.

He told how he had been looking forward to the weekend family reunion, how his entire family had piled into a family van and were on the way to pick him up when this tragic accident occurred which burned his entire family to death. He shared the shock and the numbness, the utter disbelief of suddenly being a single man, of having had children and suddenly becoming childless, of living without a single close relative. He told of his total inability to come to grips with it. He shared how he changed from a money-earning, decent, middle-class husband and father to a total bum, drunk every day from morning to night, using every conceivable drug and trying to commit suicide in every conceivable way, yet never able to succeed. His last recollection was that after two years of literally bumming around, he was lying on a dirt road at the edge of a forest, drunk and stoned as he called it, trying desperately to be reunited with his family. Not wanting to live, not even having the energy to move out of the road when he saw a big truck coming toward him and running over him.

It was at this moment that he watched himself in the street, critically injured, while he observed the whole scene of the accident from a few feet above. It was at this moment that his family appeared in front of him, in a glow of light with an incredible sense of love. They had happy smiles on their faces, and simply made him aware of their presence, not communicating in any verbal way but in the form of thought transference, sharing with him the joy and happiness of their present existence.

This man was not able to tell us how long this reunion lasted. He was so awed by his family's health, their beauty, their radiance and their total acceptance of this present situation, by their unconditional love. He made a vow not to touch them, not to join them, but to re-enter his physical body so that he could share with the world what he had experienced. It would be a form of redemption for his two years of trying to throw his physical life away. It was after this vow that he watched the truck driver carry his totally injured body into the car. He saw an ambulance speeding to the scene of the accident, he was taken to the hospital's emergency room and he finally re-entered his physical body, tore off the straps that were tied around him and literally walked out of the emergency room. He never had delirium tremens or any aftereffects from the heavy abuse of drugs and alcohol. He felt healed and whole, and made a commitment that he would not die until he had the opportunity of sharing the existence of life after death with as many people as would be willing to listen. It was after reading a newspaper article about my appearance in Santa Barbara that he sent a message to the auditorium. By allowing him to share with my audience he was able to keep the promise he made at the time of his short, temporary, yet happy reunion with his entire family.

We do not know what happened to this man since then, but I will never forget the glow in his eyes, the joy and deep gratitude he experienced, that he was led to a place where, without doubt and questioning, he was allowed to stand up on the stage and share with a group of hundreds of hospice workers the total knowledge and awareness that our physical body is only the shell that encloses our immortal self.

-- Near-Death Experience Researcher Elisabeth Kubler-Ross

− Ten −
Hell

While most near-death experiences are pleasant, a small percentage of NDEs are very disturbing. Instead of visiting heavenly realms, experiencers visit hellish ones like those described in Plato's Republic, the Tibetan Book of the Dead, and Dante's Inferno. What are these frightening realms, why do people end up in them, and how can they be avoided and/or escaped from should we find ourselves in one? Hellish experiences have a lot to teach us. We would be wise to take these experiences seriously and listen carefully to the penetrating insights and helpful advice that people who have visited these dark realms offer us...

294

The most frightening things that I have encountered in my life were not from fictional books or scary movies, but from near-death experiences with hellish content.

-- Near-Death Experience Researcher Jeffrey Long, MD

295

Hellish NDEs may describe landscapes, entities, or sensations that are unworldly, frightening, and suggestive of classical concepts of hell. Hellish NDEs are a relatively small percentage of all frightening NDEs. It is estimated that about one percent of all NDEs shared with NDERF are hellish.

-- Near-Death Experience Researcher Jeffrey Long, MD

296

It is often difficult for near-death experiencers to find the words to describe their pleasant experiences. It is understandable how even more difficult it would be for an NDEr to share an experience that was frightening or even terrifying. NDErs experiencing hellish NDEs are likely aware that they risk negative judgments from others due to the content of their NDEs.

-- Near-Death Experience Researcher Jeffrey Long, MD

297

As with heaven, near-death experiencers have witnessed numerous variations of hell realms. These hell realms are not for judgment, nor punishment, nor are they eternal. They are states of mind which act as a "time out" condition for reflection, education, and purification of negative thought patterns. We can also witness numerous manifestations of these hell realms right here on Earth. You can see people rotting away in prison; alcoholics passed out on Skid Row; addicts out of their minds in crack houses; people killing each other out of hatred; unsatisfied people living in luxury; all kinds of hellish conditions involving unnecessary suffering. While hell realms can be seen on Earth, they are merely a reflection of the inner hell within people. Hell realms in the spirit world are the perfect outward manifestation of the inner hellish condition within people. This is because when we die, we "step into" the inner spirit realm we have cultivated within us our entire life. And because time does not exist in the spirit realms, a person's stay in these realms can seem like an eternity or a second. People in these hellish spirit realms remain in this condition for however long best serves their spiritual development. The way out of these hellish realms is to have a willingness to see the light and seek love. Eventually, like prodigal sons, every suffering soul in these hellish realms will see the light and heaven.

-- Near-Death Experience Researcher Kevin Williams

298

I went to hell and returned. And through the subsequent weeks, months, and years, I periodically returned to hellish states of mind. Not only I, but you probably make frequent trips to hell, too -- in your feelings, thoughts, and mental conceptions. We enter hell many times through conflicts, arguments, and depressions, during which our mental state escalates into heated emotion or frozen despair. These states of mind are a glimpse into the complete universe of hell.

-- Near-Death Experiencer Samuel Bercholz

299

Hell is a psychological condition, which represents the hellish inner thoughts and desires within some souls. In hell, souls become uninhibited and their hellish condition is fully manifested.

-- Near-Death-Like Experiencer Emanuel Swedenborg

300

Hell, while also a specific dimension, is primarily a state of mind. When we die, we are bound by what we think . . . I had been in hell long before I died, and I hadn't realized it because I had escaped many of the consequences up until the point that I took my life. But when we die, our state of mind grows far more obvious because we are gathered together with those who think as we do.

-- Near-Death Experiencer Angie Fenimore

301

Almost all who come into the next life think that hell is the same for everyone, and Heaven is the same for everyone, when in reality there are unlimited variations in either case. Hell is never exactly the same for one person as for another, nor is Heaven, just as there is never one person, spirit, or angel who is exactly the same as another.

-- Near-Death-Like Experiencer Emanuel Swedenborg

302

Earlier in my life, I had read a few pages of Dante's Inferno, but I didn't continue, because I surmised that it was merely Dante's allegorical fantasy. In many Buddhist texts there are extensive descriptions of hell realms; I always avoided these sections, just turning past these pages, thinking that they were merely religious nonsense designed to scare peasants. The notion of hell was not something that my parents ever talked to me about, and I never gave much thought to it.

-- Near-Death Experiencer Samuel Bercholz

303

Though I had no eyes, a world appeared before me. My consciousness expanded from the tiny strings of light and into a complete cosmos made of sulfurous gases. Here was an alternative world, thoroughly different from the earthly world I had left behind. My senses were overwhelmed by the unbearable odor of burning flesh and extremes of heat and cold beyond imagination.

Amid these intense sensations, a second display arose in shimmering waves of agonizing pain -- the images of contorted faces, writhing bodies and ghastly body parts, festering entrails, disembodied thumbs and noses, tormented animals of every kind, some of them ripped into pieces, and even ants and other insects whose extreme suffering was palpable to me. All of them -- all of it -- was a mass of unspeakable pain. With the constant mirage-like wavering of images, I could not discern anything as either real or unreal.

-- Near-Death Experiencer Samuel Bercholz

304

What I saw horrified me more than anything I have ever seen in life. Since you could tell what the beings of this place thought, you knew they were filled with hate, deceit, lies, self-righteousness bordering on megalomania, and lewd sexual aggressiveness that were causing them to carry out all kinds of abominable acts on each other. This was breaking the heart of the Son of God standing beside me. Even here were angels trying to get them to change their thoughts. Since they could not admit there were beings greater than themselves, they could not see or hear them. There was no fire and brimstone here; no boxed-in canyons, but something a thousand times worse from my point of view. Here was a place totally devoid of love. This was HELL!

-- Near-Death Experiencer George Ritchie, MD

305

I remember seeing my body from above and having no physical feeling at all. I was then sucked downward into an unending tunnel or a vortex. It was very dark and there were red and orange flames everywhere. I was aware that I was dying and was frantic, but could not escape and come back or wake up. There was the strongest emotional and spiritual feeling of being oppressed in every possible way. It is almost unexplainable how much emotional pain I felt. It was almost as if every negative feeling I had ever felt in my life were being forced on me at once.

Flashes of my past and terrible choices and mistakes I had made flew by me. I also saw faces of my family members, they were all crying. I knew I was going to hell, and it was a million times worse than I had ever imagined. There was no physical pain but I was being tortured emotionally for everything wrong I had ever done in life. In the spiritual world, this seemed to go on for many years, yet I was somehow aware that it was only minutes on earth. I remember being sorry for all the things I had done and having complete regret. I then was pulled out of the tunnel and hovered in light. I heard someone who, I believe, was God. He was telling me I was being saved and given a second chance at life. I immediately felt peace and could feel my body again.

-- Near-Death Experiencer Ellen F

306

It was an experience I was not prepared for. I was presented with a terrifying sight that produced a feeling that literally rattled my whole being. I tried to cover my eyes to avoid looking at what had just unfolded before me, but to no avail. There was no way to avoid seeing or to hide from that which is ultimately, the reality. At my right, a few feet away, stood something that resembled a demon. It was not your average demon, but one made of cardboard. It looked absolutely ridiculous! I knew that whatever I was seeing was not real in the sense of being an individual consciousness. It was a product of my own mind. One part of me wanted to laugh at it; another part of me however wanted to scream in terror. I had never imagined a demon made of cardboard before, but it indeed had a terrifying effect on me. "So, you thought it was that easy, huh?" the demon snarled, as it came bouncing towards me. "Oh, I know what this is," I thought. This is my fear manifested: This is my own loathing. This is my lack of appreciation for life and the people in it. This is a learned experience as I walked through life, becoming more and more engulfed in despair. The demon is showing me how I treat myself and others when I am affected by the feeling of fear. This is exactly the tone of voice that belongs to me, when I am being mean towards myself and others. Here it is, manifested as my own personal version of hell.

-- Near-Death Experiencer Angela M

307

The hell of hells is knowing you were your own devil.

-- Near-Death Experiencer Arthur Yensen

308

I knew that I was going to be there forever . . . As I looked over my life, I thought about what a failure I had been. I had not been a good husband. I had not been a good father. I had not been a good teacher. The reason why I wasn't is because I was always obsessed with what's in it for me. I was not the great artist that I had hoped to be. I was just a mediocre artist, at a mediocre university. Everything looked so bleak, and I was saying why was I ever born to end up in this place of horror and torment and now just abject hopelessness and loneliness? I knew that I belonged there. There was absolutely no sense that they got the wrong guy, or I'm innocent. I knew that the people who had attacked me earlier had been people like me. I'm not proud of this, I'm really ashamed of this, but there was a spiritual affinity between them and me. They were like soul mates. My only hope in this place was to somehow become one of them and no longer be their victim, but I didn't want to do that either because I hated them, and I hated what they stood for, and I hated their darkness and their cruelty.

-- Near-Death Experiencer Howard Storm

309

Hell is a spiritual condition we create by being away from God until we choose to return to God. Hell is a spiritual condition that is totally devoid of love.

-- Near-Death Experiencer Sandra Rogers

310

My experience showed me that there are characteristics common to all the beings of hell: they possess a thoroughgoing materialism, combined with nihilism to varying degrees, and attitudes of hatred, disdain, and utter lack of concern or caring for other beings.

-- Near-Death Experiencer Samuel Bercholz

311

The "hell" that I experienced was the pain, anguish, hurt, and anger that I had caused others, or that I suffered as a result of my actions/words to others. "Hell" was what I had created for myself and my own soul through turning my back on unconditional love, compassion, and peace.

-- Near-Death Experiencer Tina

312

I found myself falling down a very dark tunnel. Demons appeared around me, and though I was spirit, they were going through the motions of ripping my flesh off. It was intensely painful . . . I woke up about 10 hours later in the ICU. I tried to talk but was unable to because of the ventilator. Eventually the doctors reversed my condition, and mostly out of danger, I stayed in the ICU for another week. While I was there, they suggested I go to addiction treatment and also recommended I address what I had told them had happened to me when I had died. They did not believe there was a hell. After that, I did go into treatment and now I have 18 years of sobriety. I became an Addiction Specialist, trying to help others learn to deal with addiction, so they would never have to experience the misery that I had . . . Before this experience I did not care about anyone. I was a nurse with no compassion (except when caring for people in hospice). Nowadays, I care very much about my fellow man and try to help whenever possible.

-- Near-Death Experiencer Frances Z

313

Men and women of all ages, but no children, were standing or squatting or wandering about on the realm. Some were mumbling to themselves. The darkness emanated from deep within and radiated from them in an aura I could feel. They were completely self-absorbed, every one of them too caught up in his or her own misery to engage in any mental or emotional exchange. They had the ability to connect with one another, but they were incapacitated by the darkness . . . The way out of these hellish realms is to have a willingness to see the light and seek love for others and God.

-- Near-Death Experiencer Angie Fenimore

314

The Less-Than-Positive Experience (LTP) is a spiritual wake-up call, causing the person to stop, look back, and review past choices. It can help him or her understand the consequences of those choices, reevaluate thought patterns and "glitches" in thinking or reasoning, and then make necessary changes where indicated. The LTP becomes the nexus point of that individual's path, causing him or her to change their walk and direction.

-- Near-Death Experience Researcher Barbara R. Rommer, MD

315

Not only do I believe that it is the person who causes the LTP to happen, but he or she is also responsible for the type of imagery that occurs in the experience and the total content of it. In the LTP, we see what we need to see, hear what we need to hear, and feel what we need to feel in order to do those reevaluations.

-- Near-Death Experience Researcher Barbara R. Rommer, MD

316

Many prior NDE studies used the term "negative" to describe NDEs that were frightening or hellish. I prefer a different label for the hellish NDEs I've studied. Personally, I call them "a walk through the Valley of Death." It is good to remember that most of these are just that, a walk through the valley followed by a new earthly life that may be made more positive by these brief glimpses of that place called hell.

-- Near-Death Experience Researcher Jeffrey Long, MD

317

There is historical literary evidence that past saints and holy men and women have experienced descent into hell. And although this brush with evil may be hard on them, it also often provides the grist for a deeper spirituality, one that moves them to greater spiritual wholeness. That is why I prefer not to think of these hellish NDEs as negative. Rather, they are frightening experiences that can lead to the same level of positive transformation as those NDEs that might be described as pleasant.

-- Near-Death Experience Researcher Jeffrey Long, MD

318

While hellish experiences tend to be very unpleasant in the beginning, over time, as people strive to understand and integrate them, they turn out to be deeply positive and transformative. That's not emphasized enough. Nor is the overriding, corresponding lesson: all of the challenges we face in life (including visits to hell) are gifts that are designed to help us become better, deeper, more full-blown beings.

-- Near-Death Experience Researcher David Sunfellow

319

It is tempting to think that a "mean" person will necessarily have a frightening or hellish experience, and a gentle, kind person will have a blissful experience. Please believe me, that is absolutely not the case. Everyone has the potential of having a LTP (Less-Than-Positive Experience).

-- Near-Death Experience Researcher Barbara R. Rommer, MD

320

After death, people gravitate into homogenous groups according to the rate of their soul's vibrations . . . In the hereafter, each person lives in the kind of Heaven or hell that he prepared for himself while on Earth.

-- Near-Death Experiencer Arthur Yensen

321

If you threw a small pebble into a threshing machine, it would go into the box -- not because it is good or bad, but because of its proper size and weight. It's the same way here. No one sends you anywhere. You are sorted by the high or low vibrations of your soul. Everyone goes where he fits in! High vibrations indicate love and spiritual development, while low vibrations indicate debasement and evil.

-- Near-Death Experiencer Arthur Yensen

322

When I asked what a person should do while on Earth to make it better for him when he dies, [my guide] answered, "All you can do is to develop along the lines of unselfish love. People don't come here because of their good deeds, or because they believe in this or that, but because they fit in and belong. Good deeds are the natural result of being good, and bad deeds are the natural result of being bad. Each carries its own reward and punishment. It's what you are that counts!"

-- Near-Death Experiencer Arthur Yensen

323

[Hell is] a place where everyone retains their physical desires without a way to satisfy them. For example, the glutton can't eat because he has no physical body. The alcoholic can't drink for the same reason, neither can the smoker smoke, nor the drug addict get a fix. The miser can't protect his money, and the sex-maniac, who doesn't believe in love, finds it impossible to satisfy his lust. Hell is a real hell for anyone who lives only to satisfy his selfish desires.

-- Near-Death Experiencer Arthur Yensen

324

The first-person glimpses of hell . . . made an unforgettable impact like no other. It's not that I perceived them as a scary warning to change my ways. Rather, the very ordinariness of hell was impressed on me -- the recognition that the hellish inclinations of the ordinary mind are not reserved for exceptionally bad people. Above all, it was a lesson in the importance of kindness -- a lesson almost too simple to seem significant, yet it holds the key to a happy life, and even to liberation itself.

-- Near-Death Experiencer Samuel Bercholz

325

The bad news is that hell exists -- within our very minds. The good news is that even the worst hell contains the seed of freedom. Hell does not last forever.

-- Near-Death Experiencer Samuel Bercholz

326

Near-death experiences make it perfectly clear that God is not sending anyone to hell. We create our own hells -- and Heavens -- by the way we live our lives, the thoughts we think, the emotions we express, the way we view and treat ourselves and others.

-- Near-Death Experience Researcher David Sunfellow

327

Highly developed souls may also have dramatic encounters with hellish realms. These experiences may arise naturally, as momentary events or extended dark night of the soul experiences, wherein souls are purged of impurities by passing -- inwardly and outwardly -- through dark, frightening, and challenging states of consciousness and/or periods in their life.

-- Near-Death Experience Researcher David Sunfellow

328

Whatever determines who has hellish experiences, one thing is perfectly clear: whatever we think, do, and feel in this world is magnified on the other side a hundred/thousand/ten thousand fold, so it's important to develop and purify ourselves as much as we can while we are living on this side of the veil.

-- Near-Death Experience Researcher David Sunfellow

329

Along with asking for and receiving help from the Divine, some NDErs also report that hellish experiences are largely fueled by intense emotional reactions. To the degree that we can calm down; take a step back and observe; make a sincere attempt to understand, these experiences not only lose their power, but they reveal themselves to be servants of The Light. If we are brave enough to face and befriend them, they offer us pearls of great price.

-- Near-Death Experience Researcher David Sunfellow

330

It's important to remember that we are eternal beings made in the image and likeness of our Creator. While it's true that we can scare ourselves (or allow others to scare us), we can't be killed, maimed, broken, tormented, or held captive forever. It is our destiny to remember who we are, what our true nature is, and awaken from all dreams.

-- Near-Death Experience Researcher David Sunfellow

331

What can be done if, for one reason or another, we end up in a hellish realm? We can remember that we are never alone; The Light, and legions of heavenly helpers, are always present, waiting for us to look up and ask for help.

-- Near-Death Experience Researcher David Sunfellow

332

To escape the darkness, you must cry out to God. Then The Light will appear.

-- Near-Death Experiencer Howard Storm

333

I began to hear noise, and what I heard was extremely distressing and eventually unbearable. As the noise grew in intensity, I realized it was voices, the countless voices of many, many souls, saying nothing, only weeping and wailing. It was the most anguished, pathetic sound I had ever heard. With every passing moment it grew until I imagined their numbers were in the millions. It was unbearable. I had to get out of this place. But how? I had no body and no voice. Finally, somewhere deep down in my spirit I screamed as hard as I could. I heard my own voice echoing on and on, "GOD, HELP ME!!!" The next thing that happened was a gigantic hand came down and moved under me and lifted me out of that abyss. I was then taken up and up. The anguished voices faded, and all was quiet.

-- Near-Death Experiencer Cathleen C

334

I had a descent into what you might call hell, and it was very surprising. I did not see Satan or evil. My descent into hell was a descent into each person's customized human misery, ignorance, and darkness of not-knowing. It seemed like a miserable eternity. But each of the millions of souls around me had a little star of light always available. But no one seemed to pay attention to it. They were so consumed with their own grief, trauma, and misery. But, after what seemed an eternity, I started calling out to that Light, like a child calling to a parent for help. Then The Light opened up and formed a tunnel that came right to me and insulated me from all that fear and pain.

-- Near-Death Experiencer Mellen-Thomas Benedict

335

Lamenting my situation, and aching for another chance at life, it dawned on me that the void is a place of my own making. A representation of my apathy; a symbol of the wall I'd spent a lifetime building. Its bricks were ones I'd stacked to keep people out and my feelings in; a barrier of my own construction, built brick-upon-brick with each hurt I'd suffered. My efforts to protect myself had made me less -- less real, less vulnerable, less joyful, as impenetrable as the coma I lay in. My physical self in the ICU had no idea how close she was to losing it all.

When I finally realized the void was a prison of my own design, it split open with a thunderous BOOM! A bright light shone before me. The darkness was still there, but now it was behind and beneath me, being pushed back and down by the brilliant light. I was being pulled, drawn, as if by a powerful magnet, into the arms of a glorious spirit. Am I finally being rescued from this terrible place? Oh, let it be so!

-- IANDS Near-Death Experiencer #7

-Eleven-
Prayer

Near-death experiences insist that prayer is a super power. We should use it accordingly...

336

I moved down through great walls of clouds. There was a murmuring all around me, but I couldn't understand the words. Then I realized that countless beings were surrounding me, kneeling in arcs that spread into the distance. Looking back on it now, I realize what these half-seen, half-sensed hierarchies of beings, stretching out into the dark above and below, were doing. They were praying for me . . . These prayers gave me energy. That's probably why, profoundly sad as I was, something in me felt a strange confidence that everything would be all right. These beings knew I was undergoing a transition, and they were singing and praying to help me keep my spirits up.

-- Near-Death Experiencer Eben Alexander, MD

337

I started to hear the prayers of all the people that cared about me. My wife, my older neighbors, my mother, my in-laws, and my brothers and sisters. I could hear their thoughts and prayers as if they were right there with me.

-- Near-Death Experiencer Anthony M

338

During my research with child experiencers of near-death states, I was continually surprised by the number of kids who saw the actual prayers being said for them, while they were out of their bodies witnessing what their loved ones were doing. They described how the power of those prayers turned into beams of radiant golden or rainbow light . . . They showed me with gestures how that beam of light arced over from the one saying the prayer, no matter how many miles away, to where they themselves were hovering . . . Once a prayer beam reached them, some said it felt like a splash of love. Others said it felt warm and tickly. Because they saw prayer as real energy that did real things and had a real effect, these youngsters went on to pray easily and often.

-- Near-Death Experiencer and Researcher P.M.H. Atwater

339

After I fell from my horse, the cowboys in the arena got on a knee, took off their hats, and began to pray. The cowboys, their wives, and their children, all these folks were praying. At that point, God allowed me to see the prayers that were coming up for me. It started out with one single bolt of lightning. It was like a lightning bolt in a thunderstorm, it started down below and it came all the way up to God's presence. And then there were two, three, five, ten, and hundred. Then there were a thousand. And once there were that many, they exploded into the brightest light you could ever imagine. And that's when God took me back.

-- Near-Death Experiencer Freddie Best

340

In the distance a gentle wave swelled up, moving across the ocean of light toward the point of perspective assigned to me. As it arose, I became aware that this wave was the concerns, prayer, and emotions being streamed toward me from hundreds of people I knew in this life and from many others who had only heard about my situation. My point of perspective rose as the wave reached it, and correspondingly, I was lifted, just a little, from the pain in my body. It became a little lighter to bear.

-- Near-Death Experiencer Cami Renfrow

341

I had just viscerally witnessed prayers, and intentions, become physical, tangible reality. In using the word "prayer" I mean something an atheist could easily do as well as a theologian -- no special form, just focused will propelled by the power of love and concern. It was made known to me that this was consciousness creating form through intention. Nothing exists until it rises into form on this field. Every single bit of material in the world -- even the computer or paper you're reading this on, and the stardust that nourishes your marrow, and the paint on the wall, and the dog you love, and each single hair on his loppy ear must have begun there on the sacred field of consciousness, shaped by the impulse of intention.

-- Near-Death Experiencer Cami Renfrow

342

I was told that the world could be saved, not by its leaders, but by prayer groups throughout the world. I was told that the prayers of a group of twenty could save a nation from war. I was told that the fate of mankind rested on our ability, individually and collectively, to change the direction of mankind in accordance with God's plan.

-- Near-Death Experiencer Ned Dougherty

343

Prayer is such a powerful force. We underestimate it so much. Prayer can move mountains if only we would let it. If only you would realize just how powerful prayer can be, you would never feel hopeless . . . No one ever prays alone. When you pray to God, there is a multitude of angels of prayer there, praying with you, regardless of your religious faith or how you are behaving. They are there enhancing your prayer, interceding on your behalf and imploring God to grant your prayer. Every time you pray, even if it is only one word, the angels of prayer are like a never-ending stream, flowing at tremendous speed to Heaven with your prayers. Nothing is too trivial or too big to pray for either. Sometimes, we get overwhelmed by a situation, such as a war or famine, and feel we can do nothing to help. We can. We can pray. When we are moved by something we see on the TV news or read about in a newspaper we should say a prayer.

-- Near-Death Experiencer Lorna Bryne

344

Prayer is powerful . . . Conscious prayer, everybody knows and understands what its purpose is. What I now understand is that all thought is prayer and it affects the entire universe, because of quantum entanglement. So be careful what you pray for, all day long.

-- Near-Death-Like Experiencer Tony Woody

500 QUOTES FROM HEAVEN

-Twelve-
Angels

If you knew -- really knew -- that angels exist and have been specifically assigned to help you (and all other human beings) become better, happier, healthier, what would you do? How would you behave differently?

345

Gradually, I was becoming aware that there was something else on that [hellish] plain of grappling forms. Almost from the beginning I had sensed it, but for a long time I could not locate it. When I did, it was with a shock that left me stunned. That entire unhappy plain was hovered over by beings seemingly made of light. It was their very size and blinding brightness that had prevented me at first from seeing them. Now that I had, now that I adjusted my eyes to take them in, I could see that these immense presences were bending over the little creatures on the plain. Perhaps even conversing with them. Were these bright beings angels? Was the light beside me also an angel? . . . I did not know. All I clearly saw was that not one of these bickering beings on the plain had been abandoned. They were being attended, watched over, ministered to.

-- Near-Death Experiencer George Ritchie, MD

346

Angels had crowded the living cities and towns we had visited. They had been present in the streets, the factories, the homes, even in that raucous bar, where nobody had been any more conscious of their existence than I myself had.

-- Near-Death Experiencer George Ritchie, MD

347

A curious manifestation after my near-death experience was that I began seeing a white glow and glint of lights around people and objects . . . One day as I was driving down a busy street . . . A delivery truck had parked on the right side of the street about a half-block ahead . . . I watched as the driver walked around to the traffic side of his truck and began unloading his cargo with oncoming traffic approaching . . . On this notable day, I watched, stunned, as the familiar dancing lights around the delivery man swirled, quickly coalescing into the form of a breathtaking, translucent, beautiful woman-spirit, glowing with light . . . For a brief moment, our eyes met. She smiled at me, then, hovering over the unsuspecting man, returned her attention to her charge who was oblivious to the heavenly presence and was busily going about his business. I was thunderstruck.

-- Near-Death Experiencer Linda Stewart

348

I glanced slowly at the vista around me, and everywhere I looked, every single person in my view had beautiful, loving spirits attending them. People walking nonchalantly down the sidewalk were accompanied by spirits. From within cars, unfettered by physical barriers, I could see the glow and form of beings around the occupants. I saw joggers with flutters of light streaking behind them as their spirit kept pace. As people entered and left buildings, light beings followed. The view before me was filled with brilliant, white light.

-- Near-Death Experiencer Linda Stewart

349

I noticed two large, androgynous beings of light . . . The angels were not only able to interact with my spirit body, but they were also able to interact with the two neurosurgeons and through them. Just before the monitor started to beep, signaling that my heart had stopped, the angels slowed down their communication and looked at me intently. Then, with great force, they said, "Watch this!" The same light that they beamed into my spirit body, they sent through the back of the doctors, through their hands, and into my physical body. While the surgeons were probably unaware of this interaction, the angels wanted me to know that they could work through them to help pick out the bone fragments from my spine; the angels wanted me to understand that my body would heal, that I would walk again, that they would be helping me energetically, and that I could call on them to aid my healing process.

-- Near-Death Experiencer Tricia Barker

350

Those first few moments with the angels stayed with me for the twenty-five years that I have worked in classrooms at the junior high, high school, and college level. I often prayed before classes that the angels might work through me to bless the lives of my students. I knew that the angels could work through me to help students just as they worked through my surgeons to help my body heal.

-- Near-Death Experiencer Tricia Barker

351

My guardian angel, she was holding my hand, rubbing my arm while I was dying, telling me "It's going to be OK, baby. It's going to be OK." That was the most beautiful human being or entity I have ever seen or witnessed in my entire life. That woman was absolutely flawless. Gorgeous. The most beautiful color skin and hair and eyes. Her touch was so soft and gentle, just soothing. You just knew who she was; that she's always been there. She's still here. And you've got one too! She's standing right beside you, holding your hand. And it's going to be OK.

-- Near-Death Experiencer Cecil Willy

352

We all have a guardian angel. Your guardian angel is there with you now, whether you believe it or not. I meet lots of people who tell me they don't believe in angels. I do. But then, I have been seeing angels since I was a baby. I see them as physically as I see someone standing in front of me. I have never seen anyone without a guardian angel. I see them with people of all religions and none, with people who are good and bad, with people who believe in angels and with those who don't.

-- Near-Death Experiencer Lorna Byrne

353

Angels sometimes appear to us as people. Angels can take on any appearance they wish. We have encountered angels and did not realize they were angels in human form.

-- Near-Death Experiencer Howard Storm

354

Angels don't appear to us in their natural state very often. They most often tone it down for us to keep us comfortable. I don't have the words to adequately describe angels in their natural state. Brighter than lightning, beautiful beyond comparison, powerful, loving, and gentle are words that fail to describe them. Artists' depictions of angels are pitifully inadequate. As an artist I am aware of the impossibility of representing an angel. How do you paint something that is more radiant than substance? How do you paint colors that you have never seen before or since? How do you describe love on a canvas?

-- Near-Death Experiencer Howard Storm

355

I have seen faces of angels of the third heaven so beautiful that no painters, with all their skill, could render a fraction of their light with their pigments or rival a thousandth part of the light and life that show in their faces.

-- Near-Death-Like Experiencer Emmanuel Swedenborg

356

Angels are with us constantly, and they are everywhere. We are never apart from them. We have angels who guard us from evil. Thousands of stories have been published concerning angels intervening in people's lives. Why they intervene sometimes, and other times don't, is between them and God. They told me that they always want to intervene in our lives, but sometimes God restrains them. God wants us to experience the consequences of our actions. On special rare occasions God allows the angels to help.

-- Near-Death Experiencer Howard Storm

357

Angels are God's messengers sent to bring you wisdom. Intuition is your angel's voice.

-- Near-Death Experiencer Sandra Rogers

358

Angels do not want to be worshipped. They want all praise to be for God. They don't want us to confuse them with God. They know the difference between the Creator and the creature. They are servants of God, created to be God's messengers. We can thank them for being that for us.

-- Near-Death Experiencer Howard Storm

359

Angels don't make mistakes, because they communicate directly with God. Their will and desire are the same as God's. We can ask God to send angels to guide us and protect us. We can ask the angels to teach us God's will. We can't make the angels appear to us or do anything that is not God's will.

-- Near-Death Experiencer Howard Storm

360

There are different kinds of angels with different responsibilities and different attributes. One angel may accompany a child, another has the responsibility for a city, another a nation, another a world, another a universe. We might think that the mighty angels are gods, but they don't think of themselves that way. They know they are servants of God participating in the divine plan.

-- Near-Death Experiencer Howard Storm

361

Angels can move through time and space as easily as thinking. The laws of physical nature do not bind angels. Angels are aware of and protect us from forces we don't know or aren't capable of imagining. Our angels are ever vigilant to protect us from evil that originates from other dimensions of the unknown universes. We don't have to worry about it. We should just be glad they are there keeping us safe. There exist supernatural beings that seek chaos. They have no power over us except the power we give them. They are known as demons, the devil, or evil spirits. They should be rejected as much as possible. The power of God and the power of God's angels is much greater than theirs. The best defense against evil is to be filled with the Holy Spirit.

-- Near-Death Experiencer Howard Storm

362

The spirit of God is the spirit of the angels. This same spirit is in us, leading us to truth and love. When we allow the Holy Spirit to guide us, we are in harmony with the angels and God. Then we become like the angels, messengers of God.

-- Near-Death Experiencer Howard Storm

363

I had the opportunity to converse with angels and ask many questions. I gained much insight.

-- Near-Death Experiencer Mary Neal, MD

364

There are angels all around us, and we each have "personal" angels who watch over us all day, every day. They help us, nudge us, and guide us in all sorts of little ways that we usually don't notice. Sometimes they push us forward, and sometimes they pull us backward. Always, they want very much for us to follow the path that has been laid out for us by God.

-- Near-Death Experiencer Mary Neal, MD

365

I saw a vision of Jesus and an angel . . . I consider myself a Christian without a denomination, and the vision of Jesus and the angel looked exactly like the paintings/windowpanes you see in a Catholic church. Jesus looked like the Catholic Jesus and the angel looked like a Catholic angel -- not a cherub, but a tall, strong, man-looking angel. The colors were amazing. I tell you all this because I thought that if/when I ever saw Jesus, He would look plainer. He was very radiant . . . I know it sounds weird, but it was like they were throwing down whammy vibes or something. They both looked very serious and intently busy with this project of theirs. I remember thinking "Hmmm, this is interesting . . . they are giving me the whammy to live so that I don't die." It was a very calm encounter, even though the physical circumstances were intense. Immediately following this scene, the doctor found my vein and gave me the epinephrine, and I came back 100 percent fully into the scene in the hospital room in my bed. All of this happened in a matter of 30 seconds.

-- Near-Death Experiencer Sally F

366

I felt like there were three angels in the room. And interestingly, they had New York accents, probably because the last movie I'd seen was . . . the original Oceans 11, the brat pack movie . . . They were there in the ICU. They probably have a regular gig there because of the issues ... They said, "Mark, you want to come with us. You know you can come with us if you want." Complete New York accent. The way they introduced themselves, they said, "Mark, uh, we're angels; we're angels down here." And established that simpatico thing. "You want to come with us?" I said, "No, I'll hold off."

-- Near-Death Experiencer and Former U.S. Senator Mark Kirk

367

Over 70 percent of children's near-death scenarios involve angels. Not that many adults claim this, more like 40 percent (although adults often use terms like "light beings" or "bright ones" as if they were describing angels).

-- Near-Death Experiencer and Researcher P.M.H. Atwater

368

Child experiencers are often met by a "critical or caring" parental type of being, seldom biologically related to them, but almost always someone the child recognizes as an authority figure they must respect (religious or otherwise). This being instructs or lectures the child on behavior and what must be done to fulfill the reason for his or her birth. These instructions or lectures can be quite stern and involve incidents where the child is judged on his or her progress toward the goal. If a tribunal is present, it is not unusual for the "judges" to be animals rather than people.

-- Near-Death Experiencer and Researcher P.M.H. Atwater

369

If only you could see the look of unconditional love I see guardian angels giving the person they are guarding, you would never doubt how special you are. You are the most important person in the world to your guardian angel, and it will do all it can to help you.

-- Near-Death Experiencer Lorna Byrne

370

Presenting my biggest argument against coming back into the world, I told them that it would break my heart, and I would die, if I had to leave them and their love . . . I mentioned that the world was filled with hate and competition, and I didn't want to return to that maelstrom . . . My friends [Jesus and the angels] observed that they had never been apart from me...

"Be still, get quiet, talk to us, tell us everything you want to say. Then be really quiet and still and invite our love into your heart and you'll know that we are right there, and you'll know our love right there."

This works. It really works.

-- Near-Death Experiencer Howard Storm

-Thirteen-
Nature

We are called to love, appreciate, and protect the plants and animals we share this world with. We are also encouraged to spend time in nature, which can help us heal and reconnect with the deeper parts of ourselves...

371

I heard a voice say to me, "You have not fulfilled your purpose here."

I said, "What is my purpose?"

And this voice says to me, "The same as every man. You were put on the Earth to take care of the Earth..."

We, as men, are here to take care of the Earth. That's one of our responsibilities. It was very personal. He said, "You're not to strip mine the Earth. You're not to pollute the Earth. You're not to destroy your home." And I was being indicted, because I was responsible. I was a litterer. I was one that didn't care about nature or the environment at all. And this was a beautiful home that God had created for me to live in and enjoy.

And [The Voice] said, "Secondly, you're here for the animals. They look up to you. You're the one with the spirit. You're the one with reason, with intelligence, with the strength to change things, the ability to protect them and take care of them and do for them. They don't have that ability. And yet you destroy species after species."

And I knew that I was responsible, partly responsible. I had hunted for sport. I had no concern for animals. I never showed any compassion. I didn't have any compassion for animals or men.

And [The Voice] said, "Thirdly, and most importantly, you're here for each other. And you -- this imperative, YOU -- I sent to be part of the answer. You've just been part of the problem."

-- Near-Death Experiencer Oliver John Calvert

372

As I was doing my Life Review, at about five years old, Spirit wanted me to see that I was very much in touch with nature as a child. Nature was a beautiful place to be, and a lesson that I needed to bring back: the power of nature is an amazing thing. The minute I thought about that, suddenly I was in this otherworldly place. The grass was so green. The light was so bright. It felt like Heaven . . . As I was walking through this grass, I wanted to come back and remind others to connect with nature; that there is so much peace, and beauty, and joy that can be had in nature. It's important to spend time -- peaceful time -- in nature.

-- Near-Death Experiencer Tricia Barker

373

At the end of my life-review, I ended up in a vividly green, lush, heavenly landscape. Much like my spirit body felt eternal, the grass, trees, and the natural landscape of Heaven appeared deeply and completely alive without a hint of desecration. I wondered if this is how beautiful nature could be if we lived in greater balance. There is healing potential in nature. I have known this at various times even before my near-death experience, but to hear the command "REMIND THEM TO GO TO NATURE" as a direct message from the Heavens has stayed with me.

-- Near-Death Experiencer Tricia Barker

374

I now perceive nature differently. Whenever I look at a tree or a plant, I notice little aspects that I never saw before. I feel how alive plants are on many levels. I notice whenever plants are sick or dying. They are precious to me, and I even talk to them. Animals seem different too. I notice how similar they are to humans. In the quiet pauses between the barks of dogs and meows of cats, I hear them communicating certain words and thoughts. And I pay attention to the purity of my drinking water. Whenever I go by a lake, I feel the presence of God very strongly. There are reminders of my NDE everywhere.

-- Near-Death Experiencer Chris Batts

375

I heard music, more beautiful than anything I had ever heard before. It was then that I noticed everything had its own pitch or sound. The trees had a sound, the leaves on the trees had their own sound, the grass had a sound, the rocks had their own sound, the water had yet another sound, and so on. And when you take all of those individual sounds and put them all together, it sounded like the most magnificent symphony and choir ever created. And what's even more amazing was everything and everyone in Heaven was singing praises to God. It just poured out of every leaf, rock, blade of grass, every bird. It was the most beautiful sound I have ever heard. I can still hear it, even now, after all these years. It is like a song in the wind. Every now and then, I still hear the heavenly music, as the breeze blows through the leaves on the trees. It carries me back there, and I feel that deep, all-encompassing love again. It heals my soul, and my spirit soars.

-- IANDS Near-Death Experiencer #8

376

It's not true that only humans have souls. Insects, animals, plants have souls, too. Yes, I still eat meat, for in this realm species eat each other to survive, but I bless my food and say thanks for the gift life gives. If I don't, the food sours in my stomach.

-- Near-Death Experiencer Berkley Carter Mills

377

The redwoods reminded me so much of the forests of Heaven that I was on the verge of tears for the several days I visited. But not only did these glorious trees remind me of my time in the spiritual realm, I began to sense something else. Call it wisdom, intelligence, or consciousness, I immediately felt as if the trees were communicating with me . . . I felt the passing of millennia when I stood in that forest. I sensed their generations of 1,000 years or more anchoring them to that stretch of coastline, while ours of a mere 20 or 30 years seem fleeting and inconsequential in comparison. One generation of those redwoods takes us back to the Middle Ages in Europe or the height of the Mayan Empire in the Americas. Another generation backward takes us to the time of Jesus or even the Buddha, yet another generation and we're visiting the Middle Kingdom of Egypt. Just a handful of generations of redwoods spans the entirety of recorded human history.

-- Near-Death Experiencer Nancy Rynes

378

I've changed from non-believer, and materialist, career person, to a spiritual believer, having contacts with the dead and not giving so much importance to how I live here on Earth. Animal rights, and the rights of the weak and poor is the most important thing to me. I fight for the weakest!

-- Near-Death Experiencer Maria TK

379

The next thing I remember is traveling quickly over the Earth . . . There were fields of crops all over . . . As I would zoom in and get close, I would be told, "This has been poisoned. The food has been altered and poisoned. It is no longer pure. The people are consuming impure food. This is death." I felt sad and concerned about this and wondered why . . . I was told that man should return to the Earth or death would ensue everywhere. It was said again and again during this scene to "Return to the Earth." I was told that upon my return, I should look for pure food, unadulterated . . . and only consume that which is "clean"...

Since that time, everything has changed for me. My health has returned. I get stronger and stronger each year. To my surprise, I found the day after this event that I felt well, except that I could not eat any meat at all. Nor did I have any desire to. I've been a vegetarian since then. I eat a lot of raw organic foods. I don't eat anything with chemical ingredients and keep my food very pure. My children and husband eat mostly this way too now, and we are all feeling great.

-- Near-Death Experiencer Amy Call

380

I was shown the problem with our food supply also. I saw fields burning and know that God is very upset about it. A stem of wheat was held up to me to see without any explanation, but a feeling of danger was given to me.

-- Near-Death Experiencer David Brooks

381

I am a more compassionate and tolerant person than I was prior to my experience. I live my life in a spiritual way with regard for all creatures and the environment. I no longer kill anything if I can help it, whereas before I was a champion spear fisherman and hunter. I am a vegan who supports animal welfare causes, and my wife and I have taken in rescued pets as family members.

-- Near-Death Experiencer Phil S

382

We ourselves -- every man, woman, and child -- are the guardian angels of our planet, of all nature. We all need to protect nature, all of the animals of this planet, as well as all the plants, and trees, and rivers.

-- Near-Death Experiencer Lorna Byrne

383

A gentleman asked me, "Do you think the Lord knows this or that?" God knows if your lawn is too dry. If the grass is too long. There is not an insect small enough or insignificant enough to be overlooked. That is a very difficult thing for me or anyone to understand. How could a Being be so in touch with everything all at one time? Trillions of things going on just on Earth, let alone the whole universe. Think of all the things going on -- the insects, the animals, the sea creatures -- but yet there is not a time when His eye is taken off any of us. It's hard to comprehend that, but through my experience, I was told that's how it is.

-- Near-Death Experiencer Scott H

384

I spoke to some of my relatives and agreed to pass messages on for them. I spoke to my animals and agreed to help animals.

-- Near-Death Experiencer Carmel B

385

I would attract wild animals like a magnet. They loved being around me (even raccoons!), and I knew they were God's messengers reminding me of how loved I am, and that I was NOT alone.

-- Near-Death Experiencer Carlos K

386

I live life with what are generally considered eccentricities, because I see what isn't seen by others. For instance, I insist on keeping part of our yard as a micro-habitat in which birds, bees, insects, wildflowers, and mammals can thrive. My neighbors only see an un-mown lawn.

-- Near-Death Experiencer Peter Panagore

387

I was in the middle of some kind of hologram. I noticed all my feelings, emotions, personality, and knowledge were still with me, and that I carried a large amount of anger toward certain people, especially my parents and the religion they used against me. I'd been an agnostic for years. Then once having this experience during surgery in an out of my body state, I suddenly observed a Being of Light instantly entering this holographic space, and when He came, I was washed with a flood of love and forgiveness for everyone and everything. I even loved the Earth and all its beauty and the animals on the Earth and "felt" the spiritual process we are all in, and how we are literally tied together as brothers and sisters needing to be unified in love and care.

-- Near-Death Experiencer Chamisa H

388

From the light came two dogs of mine. One was a collie named Mimi who had died three years previously from an infection, and the other was a boxer named Sam who had died two years before after being hit by a car. The dogs came running and jumped on me and kissed my face with their tongues. Their tongues weren't wet, and I felt no weight when they jumped on me. The dogs seemed to glow from a light that was inside them.

I recall saying to myself, "Thank you, God, for letting my dogs be alive."

The Light spoke and It said, "Lynn, it is not time for you yet. Go back, child."

I know this sounds silly, but I asked The Light, "If I go, can I come back, and will my dogs still be here waiting for me?"

The Light said, "Yes."

-- Near-Death Experiencer Lynn (age 13)

-Fourteen-
God, Jesus, Religion

If our visions of God, Jesus, and religion are true, they won't be trumpeting their own horns. Instead, they'll be focused on loving us and teaching us how to love others, especially those who are different from us and those who have been rejected, disempowered, and ostracized...

389

By comparing near-death experience accounts, we begin to see a coherent picture of this other world. For example, one striking aspect of these accounts is the consistency with which a Divine is described. Those who report meeting a Divine Being generally portray God as someone who radiates incredible love, light, grace, and acceptance. This is not religious dogma or theology, but one of the most consistent claims of multiple individuals who have encountered a Heavenly Being. In other words, people are not merely stating or projecting their religious yearnings or beliefs, but, like the explorers of old, are describing an entity they have encountered. The fact that they describe these encounters so similarly gives us confidence that they have, indeed, met the same Being.

-- Near-Death Experience Researcher Jeffrey Long, MD

390

When we examine near-death experiences as a whole; when we consider the experiences that people from all over the world, including non-Christians, are reporting, the best estimates we currently have indicate that Jesus only shows up in 6.5 percent of these experiences. What makes it look like Jesus is more dominant is that some of the most famous and influential NDEs that have been reported come wrapped in Christian packages. Western civilization, especially America, is also dominated by Christians and Christian traditions. That means that the western media and, by extension, much of the global communications network, is heavily influenced by Christian sensibilities. And this, in turn, produces more reporting of NDEs with overtly Christian themes, which generate higher ratings, produce more best sellers, and make more money than less Christian, less dramatic NDEs.

But there is another inescapable truth to consider.

If you wash away the dirt that has been piled on Jesus for the last 2,000 years and go back to the earliest records, which pre-date Christianity and the New Testament, you discover someone that is astonishingly aligned with the core truths presented in NDEs from around the world. Simply put: There is no other historical figure who embodies the core truths presented by NDEs more fully than Jesus, especially the central and uncompromising call to love one another, love God, and love ourselves.

-- Near-Death Experience Researcher David Sunfellow

391

"Have you come across any NDEs that feature Muhammad as a central figure greeting NDErs? Also, what about Buddha? And Krishna? And other major religious figures? Do you have any statistics for how often these folks show up in NDEs?"

Near-Death Experience Researcher Jeffrey Long answers:

"I cannot recall any NDEs with Muhammad as a central figure. I recently published a paper on over 20 Muslim NDEs from Iran. We found the content of these NDEs to be strikingly similar to typical Western NDEs. In dialoguing with the Iranian co-author, I asked about Muhammad in Muslim NDEs. He said that Muslims have a cultural taboo against sharing encounters with Muhammad, and thus even if they encountered Muhammad in their NDEs, they would likely be very reluctant to share that. Buddha and Krishna are rarely reported in NDEs. You can go to the Search Box at the top right of the nderf.org website, enter these religious figures, and see this."

– Near-Death Experience Researcher Jeffrey Long, MD

392

"What did Jesus look like?"

"He had a beautiful, long, white robe. And he had dark skin and a big beard -- kind of like Santa Claus, but not really -- and dark hair. And there was a sash on his robe."

"Sometimes you talk about Jesus, and sometimes you talk about God."

"Well," Annabel said, enjoying the opportunity to Sunday-school me, "they are both the same. Jesus is God."

-- Near-Death Experiencer Annabel Beam (10 years old) talking with her mother about her encounter with Jesus

393

I was standing in front of this majestic Being, of whom I had been told: "Stand up! You are in the presence of the Son of God." I had never seen such a being. He was powerfully built even in His spiritual transfigured body, which radiated a brilliant white light. I thought, "No wonder He could walk through a mob and no one would attack Him, if His physical body was anything like His magnificent spiritual body." In fact, He did not look like any of the paintings I had seen of Him in the stained-glass windows of the churches where I had been.

This was no sweet, gentle Jesus, meek, weak, or mild. Here stood a robust male, who radiated strength.

Due to the brilliant light emitting from this Being, it was difficult to make out the color of His hair or eyes, but I sensed, more than saw, that He had blue eyes with chestnut-brown hair parted in the middle. He was slightly taller than I, which would place His height at over six feet, two inches. Though He was dressed in a magnificent white robe, His powerful muscular frame shone through. He was ageless and yet appeared about 35 years of age.

All of the above description is not sufficient to describe the most outstanding thing about Him. Here stood a Being that knew everything I had ever done in my life, for the panorama of my life surrounded us, and yet He totally accepted and loved me. I have never felt such love or compassion. Before He entered the room, I was desperately alone and frightened and could only think about how I could return to my body so I might be able to continue my life on Earth. After being in His presence and feeling His love, I never wanted to leave Him again for any reason. Nothing I had, no one I had ever known on Earth, could make me want to leave Someone who loved and accepted me like this One.

-- Near-Death Experiencer George Ritchie, MD

394

This is going to sound silly, but I let it slip that I hated Christianity. And this voice of God (that felt like the spirit of Jesus) laughed! God has a great sense of humor! Then I realized I didn't hate Christianity and definitely did not hate Jesus, I just did not like some of his followers...

As I spoke with God, His love for me -- this intense love that I can't explain -- was making me feel powerful. For a little while, God let me see through His eyes. I suddenly felt love for everyone.

-- Near-Death-Like Experiencer Krystal Winzer

395

Jesus has come to me twice since my accident whenever I needed Him most. He is loving and kind and has a sense of humor. He talks in a matter-of-fact tone and is actually quite a friendly fellow.

-- Near-Death Experiencer Victor B

396

The Light kept changing into different figures, like Jesus, Buddha, Krishna, mandalas, archetypal images, and signs. I asked The Light, "What is going on here?" The information transferred to me was that your beliefs shape the kind of feedback you are getting before The Light. If you were a Buddhist or Catholic or Fundamentalist, you get a feedback loop of your own stuff. You have a chance to look at it and examine it, but most people do not.

-- Near-Death Experiencer Mellen-Thomas Benedict

397

One of the near-death experience truths is that each person integrates their near-death experience into their own pre-existing belief system.

-- Near-Death Experience Researcher Jody Long

398

I was given a tour of all the heavens that have been created: The Nirvanas, the Happy Hunting Grounds, all of them. I went through them. These are thought form creations that we have created . . . Some heavens are very interesting, and some are very boring. I found the ancient ones to be more interesting, like the Native American ones, the Happy Hunting Grounds. The Egyptians have fantastic ones. It goes on and on. There are so many of them.

-- Near-Death Experiencer Mellen-Thomas Benedict

399

The Ultimate Godhead of all the stars tells us: "It does not matter what religion you are." They come and they go, they change. Buddhism has not been here forever, Catholicism has not been here forever, and they are all about to become more enlightened. More light is coming into all systems now. There is going to be a reformation in spirituality that is going to be just as dramatic as the Protestant Reformation.

-- Near-Death Experiencer Mellen-Thomas Benedict

400

The guides taught us that doctrine, and creed, and race, meant nothing. No matter what we believed, we were all children joined under one God, and the only rule was God's true law: "Do unto others as you would have them do unto you." We should treat all people as if they were a part of our soul, because they are.

-- Near-Death Experiencer May Eulitt

401

I remember before dying, a long time ago, I was told that "No man could stand before Jesus or God." I thought, "Well, why would that be?" I mean, "Would He beat you down or something?" I never understood why they would say that. Now I know why; it is because His love is so mighty that I can't even describe it. This love is so intense that I could not stand, because it just knocked me over.

-- Near-Death Experiencer Sheila Shaw

402

I felt embarrassed that I hadn't believed in Him. And I just fell at His feet. There are a lot of examples in the Bible of people falling at His feet.

-- Near-Death Experiencer Pauline Glamochak

403

As an 11-year-old child, I didn't really enjoy a relationship with Christ. I saw Him as just the story of our religion. I didn't have much faith in Christ Himself. I wasn't really a believer in Christ.

So, when I saw Him coming towards me, I basically said inside of myself, "Is that who I think it is?" Then I felt this chuckle inside of me and realized then that was how He communicated.

-- Near-Death Experiencer Pauline Glamochak

404

I said Jesus was black, but then later I said He was white . . . He comes to you in the form you are most comfortable with. He could have come to me blue, green, or purple, and I wouldn't have cared, because the love is all that's important to me . . . In my mind, He came to me in the color of love.

-- Near-Death Experiencer Sheila Shaw

405

He looked like a hippie. He had long, wavy hair. He wasn't purfurred, you know, but He was just perfect. He had a strong jaw. He had such warmth in His smile and His eyes. He was just beautiful. He had a strong nose as well, and His lips were beautiful. That's what I remember. I don't know why I remember that so much, because He didn't talk with His mouth. I don't know if I was too shy to look into His eyes, but I remember His lips, and they were just so full and beautiful. He was chiseled, you know. He had a chiseled face. He looked Middle Eastern. He didn't look like any particular race. I know this sounds weird, but He had more of a Mediterranean kind of look to Him. He wasn't blond. What color was His hair and His eyes? His hair was brown. But you know what, to be completely honest, I can't remember [the color of His eyes]. I'd love to be able to say, you know, I saw flames in His eyes. I probably did look a lot into His eyes, but I just can't remember the color for whatever reason. It's not been given to me to remember that.

-- Near-Death Experiencer Pauline Glamochak

406

I wanted to see His eyes. When I did, Jesus looked back at me, smiling a broad, warm smile, and He was just gorgeous. His eyes were the universe, spinning like kaleidoscopes.

-- Near-Death-Like Experiencer Lisa Freeman

407

He was just the most handsome man I've ever seen. I can sit here and talk about how gorgeous He was all day, because He really was extraordinary. Extraordinarily handsome.

-- Near-Death Experiencer Pauline Glamochak

408

Jesus told me plainly that everyone is given life to learn to love. And that includes us. There were so many things that were communicated without words and without Him telling me, but by showing -- showing how He looks at us is how we should also consider ourselves. Who are we to denigrate His creation? Who are we to denigrate ourselves if God sees us as beautiful and perfect?

-- Near-Death Experiencer Pauline Glamochak

409

He explained the oneness to me; that everybody was equal in His eyes and that He died for the whole world; that it wasn't just for Catholics, or Christians. He really imbued that understanding in me.

-- Near-Death Experiencer Pauline Glamochak

410

I know that other people have not seen Jesus -- they have seen a Being of Light. Jesus is a Being of Light; it's the same; He's the light of The Creator to me, according to my experience.

He said to me, "Yvonne, I love my babies." And when He [said] "My babies," He meant "I love humanity, I love my babies . . ." It means every one of us, regardless of where we come from -- our life, our gender, our race, anything happening in our life, He loves everybody completely, and perfectly.

I said, "Oh yeah, I know, You were Jesus. You came on Earth to teach love, so no wonder." That's what I was thinking.

Then He said to me, "I'll show you how." And when He said that, He took my heart and put my heart into His heart, and we became one. And it was a complete oneness . . . we merged together, as one. For a few minutes I could actually feel each emotion Jesus had for humanity. And that's the moment I cannot express with human words. It is way beyond any vocabulary we have. Imagine billions and billions of waves of compassion, love, forgiveness, kindness, goodness, light, and purity -- waves going for Earth and carrying us through, lifting us through. It's difficult to explain that one experience. It was just beyond this world.

-- Near-Death Experiencer Yvonne Sneeden

411

I was shown how much all people are loved. It was overwhelmingly evident that The Light loved everyone equally without ANY conditions! I really want to stress this, because it made me so happy to know we didn't have to believe or do certain things to be loved. WE ALREADY WERE AND ARE, NO MATTER WHAT! The Light was extremely concerned and loving toward all people. I can remember looking at the people together and The Light asking me to "love the people." I wanted to cry, I felt so deeply for them. I thought, "If they could only know how much they're loved, maybe they wouldn't feel so scared or lonely anymore."

-- Near-Death Experiencer Peggy

412

Loneliness is often the motivation to grow spiritually. It has been the story of my life ever since my near-death experience almost 30 years ago. Ever since I experienced the fullness of Divine Bliss, nothing can come close.

In deep meditation a few years ago, I was crying and begging God to allow me to come Home and experience His Love again. He told me, "Love Me in all the people around you."

"But it's not the same," I replied.

"I am in them. Find Me there!"

-- Unidentified Near-Death Experiencer #2

413

There were three times that Jesus laughed. And His laugh is not condescending. It was a joy to amuse Him, to be amusing to Him. He's got a great sense of humor . . . And I thought, "Wow, this is amazing. This is a wonderful life." And He said, "Yes, it is." And with that, because in my heart I had agreed, and because I didn't want to miss out on this love, and because I didn't want to miss out on the experience of my life, my consciousness was projected back into my body.

-- Near-Death Experiencer Pauline Glamochak

414

During my youth I grew up believing that God is unfair. I was taught that when Jesus said, "I am the way, the truth, and the life: no man cometh to the Father, but by me," this meant that only those who publicly profess their faith in Christ go to Heaven. I felt if this were true, God is unjust, because not everyone wants, or has the opportunity to be exposed to, Christian teachings. I asked the Light, which I call Christ, how people from other religions get to Heaven. I was shown that the group, or organization, we profess alliance to is inconsequential. What is important is how we show our love for God by the way we treat each other. This is because when we pass to the spiritual realm, we will all be met by Him, which substantiates the passage "no man cometh to the Father, but by me."

The Light showed me that what is important is that we love God and each other, and that it isn't what a person says, but the love in their being (we refer to this as heartfelt love) that is examined in the afterlife. In reviewing and reliving your life, your acts, and thoughts of love bring you and God great joy, and your acts and thoughts of indifference, selfishness, and anger bring you and God deep remorse. We are all part of God's family and are all interconnected. Those organizations, or religions, which claim some singular relationship with God, claim superiority over others, or exclude people for various reasons, go against God's law to love one another as we love ourselves.

-- Near-Death Experiencer Sandra Rogers

415

When I met the Risen Christ, He wasn't impressed by what church I had joined, but asked me what I had done with my life. He was asking me if I had been kind and loving to those around me.

-- Near-Death Experiencer George Richie, MD

416

What counts is what comes from the heart, not what one professes to believe. The most difficult thing for a person who has been deeply steeped in a particular religious tradition is to realize, that the form alone is not what elevates a person; it is the heart.

-- Near-Death Experiencer and Researcher P.M.H. Atwater

417

[I asked my guide] "What's the true religion?" I immediately was inside his mind. I could see myself from his place, but also from his higher level of wisdom and experience . . . And from his place, it was as if a little kid came up and asked, "Which kind of cheese is the moon made of? Jack, Cheddar, or Swiss?" He was really sweet about it . . . he kind of smiled at me, and it was just sweet. He wasn't making fun of me or saying you're such a silly little toddler. He just smiled, and I remember his head slightly bowing and this love emanating from him. To experience myself from his view, it blew everything -- my whole foundation, everything I had come from -- it just pulled it out from under me, because now I'm thinking, "Oh, wow, the moon is not even made of cheese!" Not that I thought that, but it was like it's not even about religion.

-- Near-Death Experiencer Amy Call

418

God is love. We are all his children. No faith, religion, government, or organization we create on Earth has the right to claim their influence and power comes from Him. Even more so if they cause our fellow human beings injury . . . One more important fact you need to know. Individuals are much more important to God than the organizations they belong to. We are all responsible for our personal actions. No church, government, organization, or whatever, has a hold on the keys to Heaven. You already possess the key to Heaven in your heart, simply because you are God's child. Every religious organization that exists on this Earth is flawed in some way. Let the worshiper beware. If you really want God to acknowledge you, then find a place to be completely alone, call out to Him with all of your personal pride pushed aside, and open your heart. Think about the love you have received from others and protect that love. It is your most valuable possession.

-- Near-Death Experiencer Leonard K

419

The universe is God's Church. Religion is a cultural institution.

-- Near-Death Experiencer Sandra Rogers

420

I asked Jesus [if He had visited other planets], and He said that He has been everywhere. He's been to every planet. Not the Jesus of Nazareth Jesus. He didn't go there as a young male, Jewish guy. He went in their form. He was relatable in every world that He was in.

-- Near-Death Experiencer Howard Storm

421

I asked about life on other planets. Jesus said the universe was full of life. There was an incalculable amount of life and intelligent life on other planets. I asked Him, "What do they look like?" He said, "Here, I'll show you." And He paraded images of beings from other planets. The parade began with human-like beings and as the parade went by, they became more and more different than us. Finally, I was looking at people that looked more like undersea creatures or insects and I said, "OK, that's enough. I don't want to see anymore." It's getting a little weird. It was creepy.

-- Near-Death Experiencer Howard Storm

500 QUOTES FROM HEAVEN

-Fifteen-
Sex

God, apparently, is a lot less interested in sex than we are...

422

God is not particularly interested in human sexual expression. God is interested in how we love one another and doesn't want us to exploit one another.

-- Near-Death Experiencer Howard Storm

423

Creed, race, gender, and sexual preference have no real meaning to God. No matter who we are, we are all children joined under one God. The only rule is God's true law "Do unto others as you would have them do unto you."

-- Near-Death Experiencer and Researcher P.M.H. Atwater

424

God is really only concerned about what is within us, our heart and spirituality, not our sexual preference. The way to Heaven is through love for everyone unconditionally. We do not go to Heaven by worshipping Jesus, or by believing in His name, or by believing in the cross, or by accepting Him as our Savior. We go to Heaven by creating Heaven within us, by practicing the unconditional love which Jesus had for everyone no matter who they are.

-- Near-Death Experience Researcher Kevin Williams

425

Anyone who has grown up on a farm or ranch, as I have, knows that farm animals frequently exhibit homosexual behavior. These facts of nature, and of God, discredit self-righteous religious beliefs that homosexuality is merely a preference -- a sin or a lifestyle -- which people can easily chose to accept or abandon. Near-death and metaphysical evidence shows people are born the way they are for a higher purpose known to God and our Higher Selves. It also makes logical sense that God creates and loves everyone unconditionally no matter what their sexuality.

-- Near-Death Experience Researcher Kevin Williams

426

When I got to Heaven, one of the first things I asked was about the very issue of bisexuality, as it had caused me a great deal of concern my whole life. My lady guide walked me to a room that had a large screen in it. On the screen, I saw two forms of Light conjoining with one another in the act of making love. My guide asked me to tell her which was the male and which was the female? I said, "I don't know!" She smiled at me and said it does not matter. She went on to say that the two Lights were what God saw when He looked upon us. She explained that God always sees us as our higher selves and that gender is a very temporary thing that will not be around forever. It was further explained to me that God Himself is both a Mother essence and a Father essence to us, therefore God fully understands our attractions for members of similar genders. It was told to me (or rather I was reminded) that there are no mistakes in the way each of us were made. God knew what each of us would be challenged and blessed with. We each act according to our heart (or developed Soul center) and as we mature spiritually, we come up higher each time.

-- Near-Death Experiencer Christian Andreason

427

One other thing I was shown was a couple engaging in activities that focused on lust rather than love. My lady guide said that these individuals were in great spiritual duress and bringing upon themselves a life that would present much challenge. I saw their Soul Lights began to dim significantly, and there was a dark haze all about them. My lady guide then told me a time would come when these individuals would need to learn to come to God with their sexual selves, so that He could help them to use their sexuality in a more loving way. More than likely, emotional or mental illness would emerge and help guide them to a more loving path of expression. As I looked upon the figures, I sadly commented that lust was a major factor that involved many gay people. The lady smiled at me and explained that all fall into lust before we fully embrace the Light within ourselves. Later the lady also revealed to me that the two dim beings in spiritual duress . . . had been a married heterosexual couple.

-- Near-Death Experiencer Christian Andreason

428

Troubled by my own doubts about my masculinity since I was a teen, I decided this was my chance to ask this Being a question that had plagued me for a long time. So, I asked my question by sending my thoughts to Him, which was so natural, so easy, and so effortless, like I had telepathically spoken all my life. I asked Him, "Is it alright to be gay?" Now, I know it sounds like a strange question, that question out of all the questions I could ask an eternal loving Being, but it was sincere, and at age 22 that was my question. Today I would ask entirely different ones and not stop at one question. But the Being of Light laughed and smiled. I cannot tell you how I knew this, but I just knew it. And, with great love in His voice he said, "That is not the most important question." I wish everyone could hear the gentleness, the tenderness I heard in His voice. This is not a God of wrath and judgment. That response really surprised me, as my heart was beating in my throat when I asked it, and I expected to be given a stern lecture of condemnation. But the Being let me know that He had full confidence in me to figure out what the most important question is. At the same time I knew He wouldn't give me the most important question, that He wanted me to discover it for myself.

-- IANDS Near-Death Experiencer #9

429

If this world was to ever find out just a small amount of what sexually diverse (gay) people are here to do on this planet, there would never be one single wisecrack or hurtful remark made ever again. Instead there would be great respect!

-- Near-Death Experiencer Christian Andreason

-Sixteen-
Reincarnation

Reincarnation, like the illusionary world we live in, is one more thing that is not what it appears to be...

430

The concept of reincarnation in its conventional form of a progression of lifetimes, running sequentially one after the other, wasn't supported by my NDE. I realized that time doesn't move in a linear fashion unless we're using the filter of our physical bodies and minds. Once we're no longer limited by our earthly senses, every moment exists simultaneously. I've come to think that the concept of reincarnation is really just an interpretation, a way for our intellect to make sense of all existence happening at once.

We think in terms of "time passing," but in my NDE, it felt as though time just is, and we're moving through it. This means that not only do all points of time exist simultaneously, but also that in the other realm, we can go faster, slower, or even backward and sideways.

-- Near-Death Experiencer Anita Moorjani

431

What is my personal view of rebirth? Many of the cases that we have are unexplainable in terms of western medicine, but they are also unexplainable in terms of the reincarnation hypothesis. Sometimes you will see two children who seem to remember the same past life. Sometimes you will see a child who remembers the past life of someone who died when the child was six months old, so the two lives overlap. So, it is not a clear model we can follow. When I talk to near-death experiencers, they always say -- when they start out explaining their experience -- they say first that words cannot explain my experience. I cannot describe it for you. And then I say, "That's great, tell me all about it." So, we force them to tell us what they experience, and we know that they are not telling us what they experience; they're putting into words things that don't fit into words. And I think the same is true of the rebirth memories. What actually happens is something that we -- that our brains -- cannot understand. So, the models we come up with do not really approach the reality. So, if you ask me what I believe, I say that what happens after death is something that I can't possibly understand while I'm in this brain.

-- Near-Death Experience Researcher Bruce Greyson, MD

432

While it is helpful to conceptualize reincarnation as a process in which we reincarnate from one life to the next, when you study NDEs as a whole this is clearly NOT what is happening. What is actually happening is that there is no time, and everything is happening right now. Moreover, since we are all connected, we have the ability to pop in and out of every kind of experience imaginable, including past, present, and future lives.

Even though reincarnation is not what is actually happening, it is still a helpful concept. The perception that we grow and evolve are also time-based illusions. But while we are in this world, we don't get much traction until we understand that believing (and perhaps even knowing) we are perfect beings doesn't instantly transform us into one. Instead, we grow, evolve, learn. We begin as babies, then become toddlers, children, pre-teens, teens, young people, adults, seniors. Everything in this world obeys these laws. From where I'm sitting, reincarnation is cut from the same cloth. It's not ultimately true, but it's a helpful concept. I think it also helps to loosen the vice grip of materialism that has been strangling western minds for ages. When children report a former life as another person and can tell you many important facts about their former lives, well, that can cause even the most die-hard skeptics to scratch their heads and wonder if there is more going on in life than they suspect.

On the other hand, there are plenty of believers in reincarnation who take it too far. Instead of working to be a better person this life, they claim that they were some exalted person from another life and attempt to gain credit (and sometimes money and careers) from living off someone else's glory.

So, whether we are believers of reincarnation or not, there are plenty of potholes we can fall into. That's why I think the best philosophy is probably the one that holds concepts like reincarnation loosely and focuses, instead, on the basics: becoming the most loving and caring person we can be in our current incarnation.

-- Near-Death Experience Researcher David Sunfellow

—Seventeen—
Drug-Induced Spiritual Experiences

How can we experience near-death-like experiences without subjecting our bodies to potentially deadly traumas? Using various kinds of drugs to access alternate states of consciousness is one popular method. But how do drug-induced states of consciousness compare to actual near-death experiences? And are such attempts to access other realms ultimately helpful? The following quotes come from a conversation that took place on NHNE's NDE Network...

433

Psychedelic experiences were as different from my near-death experience as looking into a fish tank and scuba diving around coral reefs in Nassau. The only thing similar was the out-of-body experience and exploring another dimension of the multiverse. A big difference is between seeing and being. LSD showed me a mechanical, Newtonian universe. Mushrooms more of a fairy land, full of interesting, magical creatures from etheric to earthy, underground. Ecstasy was an exploration of my inner being from a loving perspective. All fun and exotic, but nothing profound, ineffable, meaningful, esoteric like the NDE.

-- Near-Death Experiencer Diane Goble

434

Forty years later, I remember no details from any of about half a dozen psychedelic experiences, but every detail, feeling, and emotion from my near-death experience. It changed the course of my life, my personality, my interests, my beliefs, my future. I know my purpose in this life, and I live it. I have no fear of death, I know what happens next! The drugs did nothing but provide a few hours of meaningless entertainment.

-- Near-Death Experiencer Diane Goble

435

The NDE experience is firmly etched and "recallable", whereas the drug induced experiences, no matter how pleasant, are hard to remember. Also, the number of people who have had bad trips on hallucinogenics far outnumber (as a percentage) the number of people who have had an unpleasant NDE. That's telling, too.

-- Near-Death Experiencer Rajiv Sinha, MD

436

I neglected to mention another drug I tried back then that I would say had a profound affect, even transformational, and that's MDMA, which became better known on the street as Ecstasy. I did it several times under the direction of a psychotherapist, and this was before it became a rave party drug and was made illegal. It was called the Love Drug, because it allows the person to move into an extremely loving state of consciousness (similar but not as intense as the feeling of unconditional love in the NDE), with the intention of resolving the past emotional issues hindering present day personal growth, including PTSD, depression, and other mental troubles. It allowed me to "see" an early childhood trauma I had repressed and to forgive my perpetrator, and express gratitude to his soul for helping me resolve this karmic past life issue. I was able to release the fear and anger and subsequently have better relationships.

-- Near-Death Experiencer Diane Goble

437

I "dabbled" with MDMA in the 80s as a drug used in therapy to help us get to issues that were so buried, we couldn't reach them but knew they were there and getting in our way. I tried it myself and became a sitter for others with the idea that they would then take their issues into therapy for at least three more sessions. For me, personally, under those circumstances, MDMA was a great adjunct to my Life Review. I was very grateful for it, and it became apparent that when those issues had surfaced, there was no longer any need to use it again. It's not recreational. It's therapeutic! I went on to work with others in the psych community to legalize it for therapeutic purposes.

-- Near-Death Experiencer Barbara Harris Whitfield

438

I want to emphasize [that after] using drugs or "plant medicine" as an aid to spiritual growth, [it is important to] be able to move on and not become dependent on it.

-- Near-Death Experiencer Barbara Harris Whitfield

439

When I gave talks in the 80s and 90s, people would come up to me (after the talk, one on one) and tell me about spiritual experiences that were triggered by other means that were not life threatening -- doing hospice work, helping someone else die, being present with a loved one when they transitioned, being present during childbirth, hearing a spiritual talk or reading a spiritual book like *A Course In Miracles*, engaging in

Stan Grof's Holotropic Breathwork, experiencing great loss, doing a 12-step program, detox, and more.

-- Near-Death Experiencer Barbara Harris Whitfield

440

When it comes to using (or not using) drugs as aids in our spiritual journey, here's a helpful question to ask ourselves: What is the purpose of life? Are we here, in this world, to leave, to escape, to enter higher states of consciousness by ignoring this one? Or are we here to become fully embodied? I've come to believe we are here to become fully embodied -- and we do this by facing and befriending the challenging forces that exist in this plane of existence. If our excursions into other realms are intended to help us be more fully present in this one (and more aware and integrated with other realities at the same time), then great; if not, if we are using them to escape this reality, then I think our escape attempts frustrate our souls.

-- Near-Death Experience Researcher David Sunfellow

441

My niece told me that God is lonely. I was stunned. I talked it over with [my husband] Charlie, and I was shocked when he agreed! I knew that before Charlie, I was lonely and what our love does for each other is support each other's spiritual growth. What we have helped each other to do is allow our soul to evolve and live a spiritual life. I can understand the "God being lonely" idea when I think of my own loneliness and how I have gotten in touch with my "God within." Charlie and I have given each other a safe place to BE . . . So when we have conversations like this, the same thing is happening . . . We touch each other in our souls. We have humility. We accept each other in all our differences and all our likeness. And to me, this is the purpose of why we are here. To grow our souls so we can realize who we are and not be lonely anymore.

-- Near-Death Experiencer Barbara Harris Whitfield

-Eighteen-
The World Is A Dream

Yes, the world is a dream. But as Yogananda wisely reminds us, "A dream head struck against a dream wall causes dream pain."

442

The light showed me the world is an illusion. All I remember about this is looking down [at the Earth] and thinking, "My God, it's not real, it's not real!" It was like all material things were just "props" for our souls, including our bodies.

-- Near-Death Experiencer Peggy

443

When I looked back on human life, it was like reading a comic book. It was not real. I was flabbergasted by how unreal human life is; how I could possibly have ever thought that I was a human being and that was life. I could not get over what kind of mechanism it must have taken to convince me that human life was real, when I knew darn well that it wasn't, now that I'm in The Light and I've got access to all this information, and I saw the truths of the Universe.

-- Near-Death Experiencer Nanci Danison

444

I turned around and looked at this world again. I saw the world that I had momentarily left. It was like so much paper mâché. It looked like two-dimensional fluff! This was the illusion, and it was all contained within this Infinite Presence. In reality, there is no separation. But in the illusion we have created here, the phenomenal world that we play in, it requires it. It's not that it is paper mâché and less than; it's just that it is required to be at this level for us to experience this level of life.

-- Near-Death Experiencer Jim Macartney

445

When I recovered, I was very surprised and yet very awed about what had happened to me. At first, all the memory of the trip that I have now was not there. I kept slipping out of this world and kept asking, "Am I alive?" This world seemed more like a dream than that one.

-- Near-Death Experiencer Mellen-Thomas Benedict

446

I knew that I'd been underwater too long to be alive, but I felt more alive than I've ever felt. It all felt more real than anything has felt on Earth.

-- Near-Death Experiencer Mary Neal, MD

447

The more I went over my medical records and my experiences with my doctors, the more I came to realize that there is no way that this brain, so devastated by bacterial meningitis, could have manufactured any of that. It should have been a state of nothingness, with the near destruction of my neocortex. And yet it was much more like the blinders coming off and an awakening to a far richer, more vibrant and alive reality than the one in this world.

-- Near-Death Experiencer and Researcher Eben Alexander, MD

448

Although it's been 20 years since my heavenly voyage, I have never forgotten it. Nor have I, in the face of ridicule and disbelief, ever doubted its reality. Nothing that intense and life-changing could possibly have been a dream or hallucination. To the contrary, I consider the rest of my life to be a passing fantasy, a brief dream, that will end when I again awaken in the permanent presence of that Giver of life and bliss.

-- Near-Death Experiencer Beverly Brodsky

449

Usually the visions lasted for about an hour; then I would fall asleep again. By the time morning drew near, I would feel: "Now gray morning is coming again; now comes the gray world with its boxes! What idiocy, what hideous nonsense! Those inner states were so fantastically beautiful that by comparison this world appeared downright ridiculous."

-- Near-Death Experiencer Carl Jung

450

It is impossible to convey the beauty and intensity of emotion during those visions. They were the most tremendous things I have ever experienced. And what a contrast the day was: I was tormented and on edge; everything irritated me; everything was too material, too crude and clumsy, terribly limited both spatially and spiritually. It was all an imprisonment, for reasons impossible to divine, and yet it had a kind of hypnotic power, a cogency, as if it were reality itself, for all that I had clearly perceived its emptiness. Although my belief in the world returned to me, I have never since entirely freed myself of the impression that: ". . . this life is a segment of existence which is enacted in a three-dimensional box-like universe especially set up for it."

-- Near-Death Experiencer Carl Jung

451

Something else that might be hard to comprehend is that there is no such thing as time! Your life is happening all at once, meaning your past/present/future are all one bubble. It's our brain (filter) that makes this so-called time linear. Huh? I know: strange! That might raise questions of free will. Do we have it? Yes and no. Just because your life is predetermined, you don't know what the outcome will be. Things can change on a dime, always remember that!

-- IANDS Near-Death Experiencer #3

452

The one thing people might be surprised about -- Roger [Ebert] said that he didn't know if he could believe in God. He had his doubts. But toward the end, something really interesting happened. That week before Roger passed away, I would see him, and he would talk about having visited this other place. I thought he was hallucinating. I thought they were giving him too much medication. But the day before he passed away, he wrote me a note: "This is all an elaborate hoax." I asked him, "What's a hoax?" And he was talking about this world, this place. He said it was all an illusion. I thought he was just confused. But he was not confused. He wasn't visiting Heaven, not the way we think of Heaven. He described it as a vastness that you can't even imagine. It was a place where the past, present, and future were happening all at once.

-- Chaz, Roger Ebert's wife, describing Roger's otherworldly experiences before dying

THE WISDOM & POWER OF NDES

− Nineteen −
Apocalyptic Predictions

If I knew for certain that the world would end tomorrow (which I don't), I would still try to love as many people, animals, and plants as I could today...

453

If you study apocalyptic, end-of-the-world predictions from around the world, across time and cultures, you discover the track record for these kinds of predictions is universally awful. They almost never happen, especially when specific dates are predicted.

And what is true of general end-of-the-world predictions is also true for near-death experiences. While few in number, those NDErs who do bring back apocalyptic predictions for the future are almost always wrong.

-- Near-Death Experience Researcher David Sunfellow

454

While NDEs have an abysmal track record when it comes to predicting global catastrophes, their track record improves dramatically when it comes to predicting future events in their personal lives. In this arena, the predictive power of near-death experiences deserves to be taken seriously.

-- Near-Death Experience Researcher David Sunfellow

455

I have been running the consciousness websites nderf.org, adcrf.org and oberf.org for over 20 years now -- near-death experience (NDE), after-death communication (ADC), and anything else not an NDE or ADC . . . Out of the 15,000+ experiences that people have shared with us over the years, the weakest evidential link is the apocalyptic visions.

-- Near-Death Experience Researcher Jody Long

456

About four percent of near-death experiencers in the IANDS Experience Registry data report seeing future world events.

-- Near-Death Experience Researcher Robert Mays, BSc

457

Jesus opened a corridor through time which showed me increasing natural disasters coming upon the Earth. There were more and more hurricanes and floods occurring over different areas of our planet. The earthquakes and volcanoes were increasing. We were becoming more and more selfish and self-righteous. Families were splitting, governments were breaking apart, because people were thinking only of themselves. I saw armies marching on the United States from the south and explosions occurring over the entire world that were of a magnitude beyond my capacity to imagine. I realized if they continued, human life as we have known it could not continue to exist.

Suddenly this corridor was closed off, and a second corridor started to open through time. At the beginning they appeared very similar but the farther the second one unfolded, the more different it became. The planet grew more peaceful. Man and nature both were better. Man was not as critical of himself or others. He was not as destructive of nature and he was beginning to understand what love is. Then we stood at a place in time where we were more like the beings in the fourth and fifth realm. The Lord sent the mental message to me: "It is left to man which direction he shall choose. I came to this planet to show you through the life I led how to love. Without our Father you can do nothing, neither could I. I showed you this. You have forty-five years."

He then gave me orders to return to the human plane and mentally said, "You have 45 years."

In December of 1943, 20-year old George Ritchie had a near-death experience that included an encounter with Jesus and the prediction quoted above. The timetable that Jesus gave Ritchie – "You have 45 years" – ended in 1988. Ritchie permanently passed over to the other side in October of 2007. The modern-day near-death movement traces back to Ritchie's near-death experience. It was Ritchie (and his near-death experience) who inspired Raymond Moody to begin researching NDEs.

458

One of the bits of knowledge that John Audette [who later became a cofounder of IANDS and its first executive director] imparted to me late one evening struck me quite forcibly. He told me that he had met a few people whom Moody had first interviewed, who all independently seemed to have had a vision of the planet's future in conjunction with their NDE. That in itself wasn't so astonishing, of course, but what John went on to tell me was of more than passing interest. All of them, he said, had had essentially the same vision and that it was one of widespread and cataclysmic destruction. Furthermore, they all appeared to agree on the year in which these events were to take place. The year was 1988.

-- Near-Death Experience Researcher Kenneth Ring, PhD

459

Every [near-death experiencer who saw prophetic visions of the future] I have talked to has given me a prophetic vision that conforms, at least broadly, to this model:

There is, first of all, a sense of having total knowledge, but specifically one is aware of seeing the entirety of the Earth's evolution and history, from the beginning to the end of time. The future scenario, however, is usually of short duration, seldom extending much beyond the beginning of the twenty-first century. The individuals report that in this decade there will be an increasing incidence of earthquakes, volcanic activity, and generally massive geophysical changes. There will be resultant disturbances in weather patterns and food supplies. The world economic system will collapse, and the possibility of nuclear war or accident is very great (respondents are not agreed on whether a nuclear catastrophe will occur). All of these events are transitional rather than ultimate, however, and they will be followed by a new era in human history marked by human brotherhood, universal love, and world peace. Though many will die, the earth will live. While agreeing that the dates for these events are not fixed, most individuals feel that they are likely to take place during the 1980s.

-- Near-Death Experience Researcher Kenneth Ring, PhD

460

Whether the Earth is shaken by natural catastrophes, or nuclear warfare, or both, Earth and the life upon it does survive. More than that, however: A New Age emerges and the devastating changes that have preceded it are understood to have been necessary purgations effecting the transformation of humanity into a new mode of being. By analogy, just as the individual near-death experiencer may have to endure the pain and suffering associated with the trauma of almost dying before positive personal transformation can take place, so the world may need to undergo a "planetary near-death experience" before it can awaken to a higher, more spiritual, collective consciousness with universal love at its core.

-- Near-Death Experience Researcher Kenneth Ring, PhD

461

This being showed me the development of humankind from the beginning of time to some point in the future. This was shown in a holographic sense; in a way that we cannot really perceive in this plane of existence. I perceived, as an archetypal individual, the stages of mankind's development. It was as though I was some sort of time traveler, experiencing life in the various stages of man's development, as if I were one of them, living amongst them. I felt the Neanderthal -- how brutish, dark, needy, and self-centered man was at that particular stage of existence. I felt the conniving politicality of the Romans who thought they were all-powerful in the days of Christ. I felt the great surge of hope surrounding the development of the scientific revolution during the time of the Renaissance. I was impressed with the importance of our new rationality. Then I moved to the current time...

I became aware that now, in this age, we exist on the precipice of the greatest choice, and the greatest step in our development as a human race. This is the most critical point in our evolution that has ever occurred on the face of this planet. We now have to make the choice as individuals and as a people, to establish unity, peace, and harmony throughout the world. Human beings HAVE to learn how to live together peacefully. Humanity MUST deal with all the obstacles to unity before a new era of universal peace will come. This is the step where we humans will learn how to become truly spiritual human beings on this earth.

-- Near-Death Experiencer Reinee Pasarow

462

I then saw that there was a small group of people who I knew to be THE JUST -- this was the title in words. These people, The Just, were working diligently, striving to bring about peace and unity, to bring about a new way of being and relating. They were trying to develop a new spiritual-social reality which is sorely needed at this point in time. They were striving to bring hope to the world. These people were not powerful. They were not wealthy. They did not have tremendous institutions or powers of influence. They were young and struggling.

In the process of their struggle to build a new civilization, simultaneously with this wonderful process, there was a great chaos and destruction going throughout the world. People were becoming more and more divided along lines of nationality, skin color, economics, politics, gender, and religion. I saw people holding on passionately to their divisive ideas. People began to polarize, to fight, and wage wars all over the world and to be filled with hatred. There was great destruction of our moral fiber and our love for one another. I saw all of our systems and institutions breaking down into chaos: governments, our educational systems, religious institutions, financial, medical, scientific -- all of these systems were breaking down to the point that society was becoming reduced to bands of people acting like ravenous wolves. People were roving the streets filled with hatred, selfishness, and darkness. This terrible sense of division and polarization, especially of race and religion, evolved to the point that every religion was fighting every other religion on the face of the planet -- except for the religion of The Just.

-- Near-Death Experiencer Reinee Pasarow

463

The vision of the future I received during my near-death experience was one of tremendous upheaval in the world as a result of our general ignorance of TRUE reality. The ultimate reality is our spiritual reality -- that constant, lasting, abiding reality that doesn't change with the whims, fancies, and vicissitudes of the human world. I was informed that humanity was breaking the laws of the universe, and as a result of this would suffer. The suffering was not due to vengeance of an indignant God, but rather like the pain one might suffer as a result of arrogantly defying the law of gravity. It was to be an inevitable, educational cleansing of the Earth that would creep up upon its inhabitants, who would try to hide blindly in the institutions of politics, science, and religion. Humanity, I was told, was consumed by the cancers of arrogance, materialism, racism, selfishness, greed, chauvinism, and separatist thinking. I saw sense turning to nonsense, and calamity, in the end, turning to providence.

With this destruction came the destruction of our physical environment, because we were totally unaware of our impact upon physical reality. Along with this great polarization and division among the people, I also saw a great breakdown in love, and that brought a great breakdown of our natural systems. First a hole appeared in the sky, and then the sky broke. The earth began to fracture, to break apart, reflecting the polarization and breaking apart of human society. The sky, and then the earth, broke and shattered as a result of our toxic and polluted hearts. Love is so VERY CRITICAL to our wellbeing as a people, and a lack of it only brings destruction.

At the end of this general period of transition, humanity was to be "born anew" with a new sense of our place in the universe.

The birth process, however, as in all kingdoms, was exquisitely painful. Humanity would emerge humbled yet educated, peaceful, and, at last, unified.

-- Near-Death Experiencer Reinee Pasarow

464

Saved by The Light was published in 1994. It chronicles Dannion Brinkley's first two near-death experiences. In that book, Brinkley claims he was shown (and wrote down) 117 future events. "For three years," he writes, "nothing happened. Then in 1978, events that I had seen in the boxes began to come true. In the eighteen years since I died and went to this place, ninety-five of these events have taken place." Many of the graphic predictions in Brinkley's book clearly did NOT come to pass, including "the end of America as a world power" due to "two horrendous earthquakes" that were predicted to unleash their wrath "before the end of the century." So, what are we to make of Brinkley and his bold declarations? Near-Death Experience Researcher Raymond Moody provides a helpful overview:

"I met Dannion in 1976, several months after he barely survived being struck by lightning. He told me that while he had been on the verge of death, he entered a realm of light and found himself in the company of luminescent beings. He said these beings had shown him a series of encapsulated visions that he described almost as though they had been film clips. He had been given to understand that they were visual representations of events that were to take place in the future.

"Many prophets seem to foresee mostly drastic kinds of unpleasantness, and the majority of Dannion's foreseeings were the typical soothsayer-fare -- looming famine, war, economic depression, social disarray.

"In the mid-1970s, when I first heard these foretellings, I was smug. As an avid, in-depth follower of current events, I felt sure the world was in for a big shake-up, a conclusion I based on simple extrapolation from the bad news of those days -- the nuclear arms race, rampant poverty in the third world, carelessness about the environment, and burgeoning overpopulation -- not on psychic warnings. I also knew enough about psychiatry to perceive that most Americans were hiding their heads in the sand about global developments. And I had heard several other near-death experiencers recite their own awesome, end-time visions of gloom and doom that were parallel to Dannion's. I surmised that sometimes, when people realized that they were on the verge of death, their defensive structures collapsed, and their thoughts raced ahead from what was then the state of world affairs to make likely inference: a worldwide calamity was in the offing.

"Subsequently, however, I admit I have been a bit unsettled by the uncanny accuracy of some of those experiencer's forecasts. In 1975, my friend Vi Horton correctly foretold (from her near-death vision) the exact year, nature, and outcome of the revolution in South Africa. And in April of 1976, Dannion told me that in his vision he had foreseen that in 1990 there would be a breakdown of the Soviet Union and that there would be food riots there. I recall that incident so vividly because what he said struck me as silly and absurd; I took his seriousness about the pronouncement as evidence that the bolt of electricity had disrupted his brain circuitry. Imagine my surprise fourteen years later when the event transpired just as he had forespoken it. There have been many other instances, too, when he issued predictions that seemed totally off the wall at the time, only to be fulfilled later with chilling precision.

"Then I must go on immediately to add that I have seen and heard him pronounce many other prophecies, detailing even the exact day, month, or year of their forthcoming, and all in the same preemptory voice and manner of all-confident authority, that never did materialize as he said they would."

– Near-Death Experience Researcher Raymond Moody, MD, commenting on Near-Death Experiencer Dannion Brinkley's prophetic track record

465

When I wrote my book, *Heading Toward Omega* (1984), I thought I knew where we were heading as a species -- toward the kind of evolution suggested by Teilhard de Chardin's Omega Point. I argued that NDEs and other transcendent experiences were going to function as catalysts for the evolution of consciousness and speculated about human beings becoming a new species. But eventually I grew doubtful about my earlier roseate optimism since the world simply continued on its benighted way, with seemingly increasing mayhem and endless wars while NDEs became only a cultural oddity. The world we or our children face is truly terrifying. But why should we believe that out of the ashes, a phoenix of civilizational rebirth will occur with a glorious outcome? Perhaps we are not destined for greatness but doomed to an ignominious end. Which is really more likely? And how can we know? If I were to write my book, *Heading Toward Omega*, in the light of what I personally am inclined to think the future of humanity will be, I would now be tempted to call it *Heading Toward Oblivion*.

-- Near-Death Experience Researcher Kenneth Ring, PhD

466

While few in number, some near-death experiencers are shown apocalyptic visions of the future. Earthquakes and tsunamis rage across the Earth. Governments and civilizations collapse. Vast numbers of plants, animals, and people die.

Other near-death experiencers are shown that the worst is behind us. We are now on a path where everything is going to get better and better.

While the specifics and severity of end-of-the-world predictions differ in NDEs, there is one thing they all agree on: a new world is coming; Heavenly states of consciousness will eventually manifest in this world.

-- Near-Death Experience Researcher David Sunfellow

467

The deepest, most profound near-death experiences tend to be lighthearted and full of hope. There is a playfulness and sense of humor to these NDEs. Instead of raining down fire and brimstone, these NDEs are full of laughter, merriment, and gentle admonitions to lighten up and not take life so seriously.

How can these NDEs be so cheerful when so many apocalyptic possibilities are knocking on our collective door? One answer is that the higher realms know the world is a dream, no one is really hurt or lost, and everything is unfolding as it should. Higher states of consciousness also know that everything works out in the end, one way or another.

-- Near-Death Experience Researcher David Sunfellow

468

The challenges we face in this world are similar to the challenges we face in dreams. After a dream has run its course, we wake up, unscathed. And so do all of our dreaming friends. Even nightmares that are hyper-real and super scary come and go.

-- Near-Death Experience Researcher David Sunfellow

469

Whether the world follows a rough path to higher states of consciousness, or a gentle one, we can help by staying connected to the parts of ourselves that know everything is OK. Instead of getting caught up in the drama of life and injecting more fear, instability, and despair into the collective consciousness of the planet, we can train ourselves to stay calm and connected.

-- Near-Death Experience Researcher David Sunfellow

470

Staying calm and collected is not simply a way to maintain inner peace, it's also a way to find practical solutions to life's many challenges. So, whatever is happening in your personal life, or in the world at large, I encourage you to go deeper and higher. Engage life, full on, but don't take things too seriously. Be cheerful and lighthearted. Joke and laugh. Be a force of nature that not only stops fear in its tracks but turns the tide and lifts others to higher ground.

-- Near-Death Experience Researcher David Sunfellow

-Twenty-
Creating Heaven On Earth

How can we create Heaven on Earth?
By loving everyone and everything, including ourselves,
as God does...

471

The world that they showed me in the near future, in a couple hundred years from now, is a world that is difficult for me to understand or accept. What I saw had no visible signs of technology. If there was technology, they hid it from me -- or it was so subtle that I couldn't even see it . . . I assumed the future would be a world of high technology and they showed me a world of not low technology, but NO technology. Where people's relationship with God, with the creation, and with one another was so intense that human beings controlled the weather of the planet -- not just for the welfare of human beings, but for the welfare of the entire planet. Everybody in the world was telepathically connected to everybody else in the whole world. People raised food by simply meditating or thinking about the food and the food would just grow. They would then pick it and eat it . . . It was not instantaneous, but it happened before your eyes. Cabbage would grow from a seed to a full-grown cabbage in a matter of a few minutes.

People lived in small communities. People could move from community to community, freely, if they wanted to. Most people didn't move around very much. Some communities put an emphasis on music. Some communities put an emphasis on science. Some communities put an emphasis on celebration, liturgy, worship. Some communities spent their time on physical relaxation and enjoyment, sports, and that sort of thing. Some communities were very contemplative and did seemingly very little. Some communities were very active and were very much engaged with their environment, sort of what we would call gardeners, but they were literally environmental sculptors, making these very beautiful places with the vegetation and the geology around them. Different communities had different emphases, but they lived in total harmony with the flora and fauna around them and in complete harmony with one another. The main emphasis of every community was the individuals in the community and most especially the children.

When people had experienced what they felt was their full life experience, there would be a great celebration, and they would lay down and die and their souls, their spirits would be raised up to heaven. Dying was not seen as a sad thing, or grievous thing. It was a joyous time. It was celebrated as a birth.

People ate simply. Dressed simply. From what I was shown, there were no possessions other than the clothes on their back and a few simple instruments like musical instruments, or tools, or things like that which were pretty much shared communally.

It was a world that's very difficult for me to make any sense of, because there was great happiness. There was very little suffering. There was no disease, because people, with laying on of hands, could heal diseases immediately. The only real suffering that they showed me was sometimes people felt a sense of separateness. And the community would allow these people to feel that, but they would pray for that person, they would surround that person with love and bring that person back into the community. So it was possible for people to move a little bit away from the spirit of the community, but they were brought back into the community. No one was left, no one was ever lost for very long. It was important sometimes for people to feel; to appreciate what they had, they needed to lose a little bit of it once and awhile.

The spirit of Christ lived in every heart -- fully and completely. It's a world that is so unlike the world that we live in. How can we ever get there? But they showed me that this is the world that God envisions for us and it's not that far away.

-- Near-Death Experiencer Howard Storm

472

We only use a tiny fraction of our brain. I understand that it is about 10 percent. Jesus said that we have abilities and powers built into us; built into us genetically and into our biology to do things like teleport throughout the universe. We could, in this world, be linked to every other intelligent being in the universe. We could grow our food by sitting down and contemplating it and watching it grow right before our eyes from a seed to an edible plant. We could control the weather in unison with everybody else in the world. All that's waiting for us. The problem is; the reason why we don't have those gifts now, why we're being held back from them, is because we would abuse them . . . We don't know how to play with the toys we've been given so far, so it's quite obvious that we are not ready to be able to telepathically know everyone on this planet. But a day is coming -- and it's not very far off, frankly -- when that's going to happen.

-- Near-Death Experiencer Howard Storm

473

[Since my NDE] I have had a deep love for all of humanity and animals. I am very sensitive to the emotions of all people even if I do not know them. I feel for all and would heal all that ails humanity and animals if I could. I know that we are all one creation and if we knew who we are and how much we are loved and valued by our Creator, life here on Earth would be

Heaven on Earth. There would be no illness, pain, death, hatred, or war. We would love and care for all others as much as we have ever loved anyone in our life.

-- Near-Death Experiencer Kathy K

474

One thing I [learned] was that we are ALL here to do an "assignment of love." We don't have to do it at all, or we can do as many as we like. It's up to us. Our "assignment" is programmed in at birth and it is the very thing or things we love most. I was such a bozo. I always thought doing what you loved most was selfish. I can remember how amazed and happy I was when this information "came into my mind." This other source of energy, using my voice, said, "That is the most unselfish and constructive thing you can do for the world because that is your assigned energy and you will be happiest doing it, best at it, and most respected for it!"

-- Near-Death Experiencer Peggy

475

The Light seems to be telling us, each of us, that we have a unique gift, an offering to make to the world, and that our happiness and the worlds are both served when we live in such a way as to realize that gift, which is no less than our purpose in life.

-- Near-Death Experience Researcher Kenneth Ring, PhD

476

Every soul is born into this world with a talent and a task, a memory and a mission; everyone arrives with a gift and a goal. These talents and tasks are Spirit-given. They are our passports into the physical realm, for when properly expressed, they assure the continuation and evolution of the physical world.

-- Near-Death Experiencer Dannion Brinkley

477

One vital aspect of our physical journey is to consciously search for and fully develop these spiritually granted gifts for the purpose of manifesting the greatest potential for the good of all. Within this particular truth lies the greatest power . . . Comprehension and conscientious implementation of this truth literally put you in control of your life and destiny.

-- Near-Death Experiencer Dannion Brinkley

478

Some of us are born to be scientists, while others may be inventors or even healers. Some among us are born to unveil the secrets of the universe, develop higher technology, or perhaps, engineer ways of living longer, healthier lives. Others of us may have been born with the blessed gift of music or art, writing or speaking. But one thing is for sure, through each of our efforts, as we put our talents to the wisest use, the world is made a more beautiful and harmonious place to be.

-- Near-Death Experiencer Dannion Brinkley

479

How do you discover exactly what your personal gifts are? More than anything else, this process of discovery will hinge upon what you most sincerely want to accomplish in this lifetime. Do you want to be a healer? Do you want to teach the eternal truths? Do you want to compose beautiful music? Do you dream of finding a cure for cancer? Or maybe connecting with plants or animals is your passion. Without being privy to your innermost desires, I can still guarantee you this: your dreams and aspirations are the real clues that will lead to your spiritual mission in this lifetime, a mission that can only be accomplished through the practical application of your inherent talents. In other words, whatever brings the greatest joy to your heart is the exact direction your life must follow.

-- Near-Death Experiencer Dannion Brinkley

480

I realized from death that actually my purpose here is to immerse myself in life fully. Not to spend it thinking about creating the perfect afterlife. I'm here for a reason. I'm here to be who I am. I'm a facet of this universe. I'm an aspect. I am the way I am for a reason. My purpose is to be as me as I can be.

-- Near-Death Experiencer Anita Moorjani

481

I was floored at how important we all are to God -- especially how important I was to God. I didn't think He knew I even existed. All the years I was beating myself up and His question to me was "Why would I go through all the trouble to make you just the way you are if I wanted you to try and be like someone else?" No one else could do the job I came here to do the way He wanted me to do it! That is why it is so important that we not be so judgmental of each other. Some of us are here to teach, some to learn and some to do both. I had to learn to listen to my heart.

-- Near-Death-Like Experiencer Mary W

482

If my journey from the bottom of a river to the heights of Heaven revealed anything to me, it is that God is not only real and present in our world, but that He knows each one of us by name, loves each one of us as though we were the only person on Earth, and has a plan for each of us that is more significant and rewarding than anything we can dare to imagine on our own.

-- Near-Death Experiencer Mary Neal, MD

483

Whoever is reading this, you are deeply loved. Your life is deeply important to God . . . Your life is critical. The love you have inside you is beautiful and brilliant and it is needed on this Earth. You can change this world with your love, which is entirely particular to you only. You have your own song.

-- Near-Death Experiencer Heather V

484

Jesus said, "Look here my child." A large book materialized. I looked into the book and it was like a flickering movie, a flickering film; like the old-fashioned motion pictures. It was the story of these people. And they were beautiful. Everybody in this story was just so beautiful. I looked in, and became immersed in this story, but I didn't recognize that it was my story until I transgressed against a friend and I really hurt her. When I saw the pain that I'd caused her, the penny dropped: "Oh, this is my life story!"

I said to Him, "What is life about anyway? I just don't get it. I don't know how to live. How do I live?"

"Life is about love," He said. "To love is what life is about."

I said, "I don't understand, because nobody lives like that."

Jesus said, "How do you live? It's about focus. If you look through loving eyes and if you focus, you can create a beautiful life."

Jesus was showing me how He sees us. So, I was looking at everything; I was seeing everybody through His eyes, and we were so much more beautiful than we see one another, more beautiful than we see ourselves. [What I was seeing] wasn't recognizable to me, because I had cast, we had cast, such aspersions upon one another and upon ourselves. Jesus showed everyone as perfect and beautiful. Extraordinarily, fluorescently beautiful. I thought I was watching some kind of amazing Hollywood production.

I knew by Him giving me this information, and showing me my Life Review, that I would be going back, and I wouldn't be staying. So, He talked to me about focus and how important that was. It's only now after becoming educated and going through all that I went through, that I understand that we can choose our thoughts, that we can choose our emotions, that we create our life by what we focus on.

-- Near-Death Experiencer Pauline Glamochak

485

A lot of people say that the world is very negative, but that's not exactly true. Look around you. EVERYTHING exists simultaneously in this universe, the positive as well as the negative. There is poverty, there is wealth, there is sickness, there is health, there is love, there is hatred and fear, there is happiness, there is despair, and so on. And there is NOT more negative than positive. It's just because we choose to see the world in this way, that it feels like there is more negative. And the more we choose to see it this way, and give it our focus and energy, the more of it we draw into our lives, and create it in our own personal reality.

Remember, I believe that this reality is created by mass consciousness. That's what I felt I broke through, during my

NDE. Each of us as individuals ALWAYS has the choice to choose what we want to see and believe as reality.

-- Near-Death Experiencer Anita Moorjani

486

The universe is only a reflection of me. If I am frustrated with the way life is working for me, it is futile to change the external elements without looking at what's going on internally. A lot of us are very negative towards ourselves. We are our own worst enemies. The first thing I would say is to stop judging yourself and stop beating yourself up for where you are in your life right now. If I am finding that I am constantly frustrated with people, and judging them, it is because that is how I am internally treating myself all the time. I am only expressing outward my own inner dialogue with myself. The more I love myself unconditionally, the easier it is for me to see beauty in this world, and beauty in others.

-- Near-Death Experiencer Anita Moorjani

487

No matter where you are, it is only the culmination of your thoughts and beliefs up to that point. And you can change it. Remember, I reversed my cancer at the 11th hour. Even when the doctors said it was too late, it was not too late. So, the first thing is to realize that it is NEVER too late to do something, or change anything. It's important to see the power that the present moment holds in turning our life around.

-- Near-Death Experiencer Anita Moorjani

488

I feel it's my self-dialogue that either elevates or diminishes the energy I radiate outwards. When my inner dialogue turned against me, over time, it depleted my energy, and caused a downward spiral in my external circumstances. I was always really, really positive on the outside, effervescent, loving, etc. and still my world was crumbling around me, and I was getting depleted, and sicker and sicker.

Sometimes, when we see someone who is really positive and effervescent and kind, yet their lives are crumbling around them, we may think "see, this being positive thing doesn't work." But here's the thing: WE DON'T KNOW that person's own inner dialogue. We don't know what they are telling themselves, inside their own heads, day in and day out.

-- Near-Death Experiencer Anita Moorjani

489

I am not advocating "thinking positive" in a Pollyannaish sort of way. "Thinking positive" can be tiring, and to some people it can mean "suppressing" the negative stuff that happens. And it ends up being more draining.

I am talking about my own mental dialogue with myself. What am I telling myself, day in and day out inside my head. I feel it's so very important not to have judgment and fear in my own mental dialogues with myself. When our own inner dialogue is telling us we are safe, unconditionally loved, accepted, we can radiate this energy outwards and change our external world accordingly.

-- Near-Death Experiencer Anita Moorjani

490

You want to know the best part about feeling this positive energy about yourself? I don't feel I even have to say anything to anyone to uplift them, but just because of my own loving self-talk to myself, people around me feel my positive presence. Without even having to say anything, you will start to notice people being attracted to your positive presence and be energized by your energy. Your positive inner dialogue helps elevate others around you, even when you are not saying anything to them, just thinking positive thoughts about yourself!!! Because energy just radiates and flows out and touches others! This is why this self-loving inner dialogue is so very important in making a better world.

-- Near-Death Experiencer Anita Moorjani

491

The most important lesson I learned about life, or what I learned that I believed saved my life, is that it is extremely important to love yourself. Very, very important! I cannot stress this enough. It was the love I felt coming for me that saved my life. I never knew before that, before my near-death experience, that I was supposed to love myself unconditionally. The love I felt in the other realm . . . the love was so unconditional. And that love told me that I was deserving, and I was worthy of being loved. And It made me realize that it's OK to love myself.

-- Near-Death Experiencer Anita Moorjani

492

Many near-death experiencers report that the unconditional love they felt from God gave them the ability to love themselves in genuinely deep, healthy, and life changing ways. How can those of us who haven't experienced God's love directly learn to love ourselves in the same way? We can study the stories of people who met God face to face and allow those stories to awaken in us similar feelings. Yes, we are humans, with human shortcomings and failings. And, yes, we are also Divine, made in the image and likeness of God. And, yes, these two wildly different parts of ourselves can live in harmony with one another through us learning how to appreciate, cherish, and fully embrace their unique contributions to our life.

-- Near-Death Experience Researcher David Sunfellow

493

I came to understand that Heaven isn't a place that you enter but a frequency that you attain. Being in the presence of White Light was "Heaven." It was the greatest feeling I had ever experienced or dreamed was possible. Having that feeling again is what I strive for -- not going to a place. The feeling, the energy I experienced became "The Place."

-- Near-Death Experiencer Teri R

494

I understood that you take yourself with you wherever you go. Your own consciousness has to change in order to experience the higher frequencies of love, peace, joy, bliss, and tranquility, which I felt a part of. So, I begged for the opportunity to do just that. I wanted to return, because I knew that my consciousness didn't mesh with the unconditional love I was experiencing. I knew that I had to become more loving in order to experience this indescribable love permanently.

500 QUOTES FROM HEAVEN

-- Near-Death Experiencer Teri R

495

When it comes to manifesting Heaven on Earth, here are the main takeaways I have gleaned from NDEs:

1 - Heaven is a frequency.

2 - In order to be in Heaven, we need to learn to vibrate at the same frequency as Heaven.

3 - The primary vibration of Heaven is love; therefore, the more loving we become, the more heavenly states of consciousness we are able to experience and manifest.

4 – It is by learning to be a loving person IN THIS WORLD that we gain the ability to live in a heavenly state of consciousness PERMANENTLY. Simply dipping in and out of heavenly states of consciousness gives us a taste of Heaven, but doesn't allow us to permanently stay in those states. This appears to be one of the main reasons we keep getting sent back to this world. We can't stay in higher states of consciousness until we have developed a consciousness that vibrates, all the time, at higher frequencies. Our souls are here, in this world, to learn how to do that.

5 - All of this is why learning to love everyone, and everything, is so important. Practicing love helps us establish a heavenly

vibration which, in turn, can be a source of healing to ourselves, others, and the world at large.

– Near-Death Experience Researcher David Sunfellow

496

I had been meditating every afternoon for the last year and a half. On this lovely spring day, upon completing my meditation, I arose with the calmness and peace associated with a lengthy meditative state.

I went downstairs to my living room, and I noticed as I looked out the window that I was one with the blades of grass and the rocks in the road. I was enveloped in a love I could not put into words. This divine love was in everything and in me. At the core of my being, I was this love and so was everyone else. In this state of grace, there was no right or wrong, no good or bad, and no judgment whatsoever. Fear was non-existent. There was no death, and I knew that we all live forever. Everyone I met was love. It did not matter what they looked like. I was them and they were me. We are all connected. The utter joy is indescribable. I knew we did not end at our fingertips. The peace and bliss are beyond words.

I became aware that a presence other than what I usually think of as myself was looking through my eyes. I had become one with this infinite awareness that simply sees without judgement. It is the very essence of life, eternal life. I wanted nothing, nor did I need anything. It was peace that passeth understanding. My family and friends kept asking me about this deep calmness they observed in me. I could not translate this verbally to them at the time. It just flowed through me and out to all . . . I realized that I needed to just live it and not try to explain what I was experiencing. How could I explain that nothing was needed, for all was given.

I recall seeing a man who was drunk and disheveled, sitting on a curb. As I approached him, I saw his true being. He was unconditional love. I felt no judgment. He was as worthy as everyone else and he was loved as much as everyone else. I understood I was seeing beyond appearances. I also understood that this is our natural state. This is how we are meant to live. It did not matter what I did or had. There was joy in every act, every chore, every occasion. Love and joy pervaded everything. The energy of the universe is love and it flows through us all. We are all a part of this love and we are all one with God . . . I became involved in helping the homeless and the hungry. I have love in my heart for everyone, regardless of what they look like or how they behave.

It is so necessary for me to be with others who have touched this depth of love. It is my hope that as more and more of us grow in truth and numbers we will one day, indeed, have Heaven on Earth. Then we will be living as all the masters have taught -- loving our neighbors as ourselves.

-- Near-Death-Like Experiencer Helen S

497

All we have to do is just love God with all our heart and the way we do that is to love each other unconditionally, because God is in every one of us. So, when I'm loving you, I'm loving God. If I'm not loving you, I'm not loving God. So, love God with all our heart. Love each other. Learn how to love unconditionally. And take care of this planet. If we all did that, we'd have Heaven on Earth right now.

-- Near-Death-Like Experiencer Tony Woody

498

The quickest way to change the world is to be of service to others. Show that your love can make a difference in the lives of people and thereby someone else's love can make a difference in your life. By each of us doing that and working together we change the world one inner person at a time.

-- Near-Death Experience Dannion Brinkley

499

"Love the person you're with. If you do that, you will change the world."

-- What Jesus told Howard Storm during his near-death experience. "Loving the person you are with" was, according to Jesus, "God's Big Plan" for changing the world.

500

Each one of us has his place in the world. Each one of us has things we need to do. And every deed that we do affects the whole world; every deed, every action that we do -- negative or positive -- affects the entire universe. That's the power we have. We have the power to completely change and affect the universe . . . Whatever you do in this world, echoes in eternity.

-- Near-Death Experiencer Alon Anava

Universal Truths

My previous book "The Purpose of Life as Revealed by Near-Death Experiences from Around the World" contains a list of 90 core truths that are championed by near-death experiences from around the world. Here is a summary of that longer list...

God exists. God loves everyone unconditionally. God has a delightful sense of humor. So do the angels, guides, and spiritual beings that serve The Light. We should too. We should also lighten up and not take life so seriously. We are immortal, indestructible beings. The pursuit of money, fame, and power do not lead to happiness. Love and serve others: humans, animals, plants, everything. Remember the little things -- the kind word, the understanding smile, the compassionate touch -- are the big things. Small, heartfelt acts of love change lives and ripple across the universe. While there is evidence everywhere to the contrary, train your mind to look beneath the surface and see the truth: life is good; the world is a beautiful place and you, complete with your human weaknesses and shortcomings, are magnificent. You are known, loved, and cherished. You are unique, essential, and irreplaceable. You have a special role to play in the grand scheme of things. When you find and follow your unique path, which is different from everyone else's, magic happens. No matter how many times you try and fail; no matter how far you may be from embodying your full Divine Nature, you will eventually succeed. Don't give up. Don't lose hope. And always remember you are never alone, even when your earthly senses tell you otherwise.

http://the-formula.org/universal-truths/

500 QUOTES FROM HEAVEN

Experiencers & Researchers Featured In This Book

The sources for the quotes in this book are documented on the book's companion website:

Quotes From Heaven
quotesfromheaven.com

A list of the experiencers and researchers featured in this book, along with the sections they are quoted in, are listed below, in the order they appear in the book.

129 Near-Death Experiencers:

Mellen-Thomas Benedict (13, 20, 160, 161, 162, 234, 235, 334, 396, 398, 399, 445)
Nancy Rynes (14, 121, 152, 280, 377)
Andy Petro (17, 87, 140)
IANDS Near-Death Experiencer #1 (18)
Beverly Brodsky (19, 41, 204, 448)
Amphianda Baskett (21, 187, 194, 263)
Virginia Rivers (22, 28, 179)
RaNelle Wallace (23, 88, 89, 129)
Peggy (24, 67, 207, 411, 442, 474)
Laurelynn Martin (26)
Laura M (27, 123, 144)
IANDS Near-Death Experiencer #2 (29)

Nancy Clark (30, 44, 109, 206, 265)
IANDS Near-Death Experiencer #3 (31, 451)
Howard Storm (32, 110, 119, 154, 164, 237, 238, 248, 259, 308, 332, 353, 354, 356, 358, 359, 360, 361, 362, 370, 420, 421, 422, 471, 472, 499)
Anita Moorjani (34, 35, 188, 198, 430, 480, 485, 486, 487, 488, 489, 490, 491)
Anne N (36)
Rosemary Ringer (38)
Annabel Beam (39, 392)
Neev (40, 46, 47, 48, 49, 50, 51, 52, 53, 54, 55)
Chris Batts (45, 120, 130, 374)
Steve (56, 57, 58)
Cami Renfrow (59, 165, 340, 341)
Julie Aubier (60, 99, 163)
IANDS Near-Death Experiencer #4 (61)
Ana Cecilia G (62, 153)
Carl Jung (63, 64, 65, 257, 449, 450)
Louisa Peck (66, 189)
Peter Panagore (68, 268, 386)
Anne Horn (71, 167)
Unidentified Near-Death Experiencer #1 (72)
Harnish Miller (73)
Geraldine Berkheimer (74)
Tom Sawyer (80, 95, 112)
Sandra Rogers (81, 128, 290, 291, 309, 357, 414, 419)
Reinee Pasarow (82, 83, 101, 103, 104, 461, 462, 463)
Alexa H (85)
Barbara Harris Whitfield (86, 105, 195, 196, 197, 239, 240, 437, 438, 439, 441)
Dianne Morrissey (90)
Mohammad Z (91, 92)
Berkley Carter Mills (93)
Shekina Rose (96)
Roland Webb (97)
Justin U (102, 106)

Dannion Brinkley (108, 464, 476, 477, 478, 479, 498)
Cecil (111)
Melinda G (113)
George Ritchie (114, 124, 134, 292, 304, 345, 346, 393, 415, 457)
Joachim Schoss (117, 127)
Alon Anava (125, 262, 500)
Yolaine Stout (132)
Joyce H. Brown (135)
Robert Bare (136)
Chris Markey (137)
Nicole Dron (138, 192)
Jeff Olsen (139, 222, 223, 228)
John K (141)
Lee Thornton (142)
Brian T (143)
Mary Jo Rapini (145)
Florence W (146)
Terry E (147)
Jo B (148)
Amy Call (149, 156, 193, 202, 203, 210, 211, 213, 214, 215, 216, 217, 218, 229, 379, 417)
Angela Williams (150)
IANDS Near-Death Experiencer #5 (151)
Ryan Rampton (157, 158, 261)
Natalie Sudman (159, 200, 201, 212, 220, 221, 271, 272)
Jean R (168, 169, 182)
Angie Fenimore (170, 289, 300, 313)
Duane S (172, 173)
Heather V (174, 175, 176, 177, 483)
Barbara S (180)
George Rodonaia (184)
Ellyn Dye (186)
Naomi (191)
Juliet Nightingale (205)

Tricia Richie (208)
Jayne Smith (209)
Julian of Norwich (225, 226, 227)
IANDS Near-Death Experiencer #3 (230)
Mary Neal (231, 232, 233, 264, 363, 364, 446, 482)
Don O'Conner (252)
Rajiv Sinha (253, 435)
Tricia Barker (267, 349, 350, 372, 373)
Hal Story (269)
IANDS Near-Death Experiencer #6 (279)
Eben Alexander (284, 285, 287, 336, 447)
Samuel Bercholz (298, 302, 303, 310, 324, 325)
Ellen F (305)
Angela M (306)
Arthur Yensen (307, 320, 321, 322, 323)
Tina (311)
Frances Z (312)
Cathleen C (333)
IANDS Near-Death Experiencer #7 (335)
Anthony M (337)
Freddie Best (339)
Ned Dougherty (342)
Lorna Bryne (343, 352, 369, 382)
Linda Stewart (347, 348)
Cecil Willy (351)
Sally F (365)
Mark Kirk (366)
Oliver John Calvert (371)
IANDS Near-Death Experiencer #8 (375)
Berkley Carter Mills (376)
Maria TK (378)
David Brooks (380)
Phil S (381)
Scott H (383)
Carmel B (384)

Carlos K (385)
Chamisa H (387)
Lynn (388)
Victor B (395)
May Eulitt (400)
Sheila Shaw (401, 404)
Pauline Glamochak (402, 403, 405, 407, 408, 409, 413, 484)
Yvonne Sneeden (410)
Unidentified Near-Death Experiencer #2 (412)
Leonard K (418)
Christian Andreason (426, 427, 429)
IANDS Near-Death Experiencer #9 (428)
Diane Goble (433, 434, 436)
Nanci Danison (443)
Jim Macartney (444)
Kathy K (473)
Teri R (493, 494)

11 Near-Death Like Experiencers:

Richard Maurice Bucke (25)
Mary Deioma (69)
Gene Goodsky (70)
Mary W (75, 107, 190, 199, 481)
Rene Jorgensen (84)
Krystal Winzer (131, 394)
Emanuel Swedenborg (166, 299, 301, 355)
Tony Woody (344, 497)
Lisa Freeman (406)
Roger Ebert (452)
Helen S (496)

24 Researchers:

Jeffrey Long (1, 2, 4, 5, 116, 286, 294, 295, 296, 316, 317, 389, 391)
Penny Sartori (3)
Janice Holden (6, 181)
Bruce Greyson (6, 431)
Debbie James (6)
Gregory Shushan (7, 8, 9)
David Sunfellow (9, 10, 11, 98, 236, 241, 242, 243, 249, 251, 254, 255, 258, 260, 274, 275, 276, 318, 326, 327, 328, 329, 330, 331, 390, 432, 440, 453, 454, 466, 467, 468, 469, 470, 492, 495)
Sheila, Dennis, and Matthew Linn (12, 42, 100)
Kenneth Ring (15, 53, 54, 77, 78, 79, 244, 245, 246, 270, 273, 277, 282, 458, 459, 460, 465, 475)
Jeff Janssen (16, 76, 133)
Barbara Rommer (33, 314, 315, 319)
P.M.H. Atwater (37, 93, 247, 250, 278, 338, 367, 368, 416, 423)
Pim van Lommel (43)
Kevin Williams (94, 282, 183, 288, 292, 297, 424, 425)
Melvin Morse (115, 256)
Elisabeth Kubler-Ross (118, 122, 126, 171, 185, 219, 224, 293)
Lee Witting (150)
Raymond Moody (178, 281, 283, 285, 464)
Laurin Bellg (191)
John W. Price (266)
Jody Long (397, 455)
Robert Mays (456)

General NDE Resources

Recommended near-death experience organizations, websites, and resources:

NHNE's Formula Website
the-formula.org

NDE Stories
ndestories.org

Encounters With Jesus
encounters-with-jesus.org

The International Association For Near-Death Studies, Inc. (IANDS)
iands.org

IANDS Groups
iands.org/groups/affiliated-groups/find-a-group.html

The Near-Death Experience Research Foundation (NDERF)
www.nderf.org

Near-Death.com
www.near-death.com

The American Center For The Integration Of Spiritually Transformative Experiences (ACISTE)
aciste.org

Topic-Specific NDE Resources

Near-Death Experiences From Around The World
the-formula.org/nde-accounts/

Historical & Cross-Cultural Near-Death Experiences
the-formula.org/historical-cross-cultural-near-death-experiences/

Universal Truths
the-formula.org/universal-truths/

What Near-Death Experiences Teach Us
the-formula.org/resources/what-near-death-experiences-teach-us/

NDEs & The Purpose Of Life
the-formula.org/ndes-the-purpose-of-life/

Miraculous Near-Death Experience Healings
the-formula.org/miraculous-nde-healings/

The Power Of Prayer
the-formula.org/the-power-of-prayer/

Heavenly Humor
the-formula.org/heavenly-humor/

Angels & Near-Death Experiences
the-formula.org/angels/

NDEs On The Importance Of Plants, Animals, And The Earth
the-formula.org/ndes-on-the-importance-of-caring-for-plants-animals-the-earth/

Shared Death Experiences
the-formula.org/shared-death-experiences/

When Loved Ones & Friends Pass From This World To The Next
the-formula.org/when-loved-ones-friends-pass-from-this-world-to-the-next/

NDEs Absolutely, Positively NOT Caused By Malfunctioning Brains
the-formula.org/ndes-absolutely-positively-not-caused-by-malfunctioning-brains/

How To Deal With Skeptics & Atheists
the-formula.org/how-to-deal-with-skeptics-atheists/

Near-Death Experiences & Suicide
the-formula.org/near-death-experiences-suicide/

Near-Death Experiences & Hell
the-formula.org/ndes-hell/

Wikipedia On Hell
en.wikipedia.org/wiki/Hell

Plato's Republic: The Myth Of Er
the-formula.org/historical-cross-cultural-near-death-experiences/

The Tibetan Book Of The Dead
the-formula.org/the-tibetan-book-of-the-dead/

Dante's Inferno
en.wikipedia.org/wiki/Inferno_(Dante)

The Divine Comedy Manuscript
archive.org/details/visionorhellpu00dant/page/n7/mode/2up

Why It's Important To Know About Shadow Issues And Work On Them
the-formula.org/why-its-important-to-know-about-shadow-issues-and-work-on-them/

Near-Death Experiences That Predict The End Of The World
the-formula.org/near-death-experiences-that-predict-the-end-of-the-world/

The Difference Between Drug-Induced Spiritual Experiences & Near-Death Experiences
the-formula.org/the-difference-between-drug-induced-spiritual-experiences-and-near-death-experiences/

Jesus, Near-Death Experiences, And Religion
encounters-with-jesus.org/jesus-near-death-experiences-and-religion/

Teaching Others About Near-Death Experiences
the-formula.org/resources/teaching-others-about-ndes/

Recommended Books & Movies
the-formula.org/nhne-recommended-books-movies/

500 QUOTES FROM HEAVEN

Notes

500 QUOTES FROM HEAVEN

ced.

500 QUOTES FROM HEAVEN

Printed in Great Britain
by Amazon